30p

A Treasury of Embroidery Designs

A Treasury of Embroidery Designs

Charts and Patterns from the Great Collections

Gill Speirs and Sigrid Quemby

WESTBRIDGE BOOKS
A Division of David & Charles

This edition published in 1985
by Westbridge Books by
arrangement with Bell & Hyman Limited
Denmark House
37–39 Queen Elizabeth Street
London SE1 2QB
© Gill Speirs and Sigrid Quemby 1985

British Library Cataloguing in Publication Data

Quemby, Sigrid
A Treasury of Embroidery Designs: Charts and
Patterns from the Great Collections.
1. Embroidery——History
I. Title   II. Speirs, Gill
746.44   TT770

ISBN 0-7135-2056-1

Designed by Malcolm Harvey Young

Typeset and printed by BAS Printers Limited,
Over Wallop, Hampshire

TO TANTE MAYA, TILLY AND JOHN
for their amazing patience and forebearance

CONTENTS

ACKNOWLEDGEMENTS

We extend our most grateful thanks to Mrs Clutton-Brock, Mr and Mrs Carew-Pole, Mrs Tritton, Sir Seaton Wills, Mr Maxwell Stuart and to Mr Lyddon and Mr Trelawnay at the National Trust; to the staff of the Textile departments of the Museums of The Netherlands; Openluchtmuseum, Arnhem; Historisk Museum, Bergen; Folkmuseum, Bygdøy, Oslo; Landesmuseum Zurich; Museum für Kunst und Gewerbe, Hamburg; Cooper-Hewitt Museum, New York; The Metropolitan Museum of Art, New York; and especially to the staff at the Victoria and Albert Museum for so generously allowing us access, again and again to study the embroideries in their reserve collection. We thank the library staff at Wimbledon School of Art for making so many important books so readily available to us. Our studies and research leave us indebted to many writers and scholars who have persued the development of design in embroidery before us.

Illustration Acknowledgements

Art Institute of Chicago, page 42, all rights reserved; *Bayerisches Nationalmuseum, Munich*, page 45; with kind permission of the town of *Bayeux*, photograph courtesy of Phaidon Press, page 18; *Burrell Collection, Glasgow*, page 32; *Cambridge University Library*, page 21; *Carew-Pole Collection*, page 53; by kind permission of Mrs Clutton-Brock; *Chastleton House*, page 40; *Cloisters Museum, New York*, page 25; *Cooper-Hewitt Museum, New York*, pages 72, 86, 115, 124; *Fitzwilliam Museum, Cambridge*, page 71; *Historisk Museum, Bergen*, page 51; *Kunst und Gewerbe Museum, Hamburg*, page 30; *Landesmuseum, Zurich*, page 38; *Littlecote House, Berkshire*, page 103; *Matthioli*, pages 78, 85 left *The Metropolitan Museum of Art, New York*, pages 57, 89, 96/7 below, 109, all rights reserved;

Montreal Museum, page 101; *National Museum of Iceland*, page 24; *National Museum of Antiquities of Scotland*, page 81; *National Trust*, pages 77, 80–1, 114; *Nordenfjekdske Kunstindustrimuseum, Norway*, page 120; *Norsk Folkmuseum, Norway*, page 44; *Openluchtmuseum, Arnhem Netherlands*, pages 67, 73; from the collection at *Parham Park, West Sussex*, page 119; by kind permission of Peter Maxwell Stuart of Traquair House, which will be open to the public during the summer months, page 84; *University i Trondheim Museet, Norway*, page 22; by Courtesy of the Trustees of the *Victoria and Albert Museum, London*, pages 35, 52, 60, 87, 92, 93 above, 102, 111 Courtesy, *The Henry Francis du Pont Winterthur Museum, Delaware*, page 123 Line drawings pages 24 right, 39 top, 41, 45, 54, 56, 59, 85 left, 99 and 103 courtesy of John Speirs.

INTRODUCTION

Standing before an exquisite example of historic embroidery is both inspiring and rewarding and leads one to ask why and for whom it was made. Where did the ideas for the pattern come from and what else was happening in the world of design at that time? These are questions that we have sought to answer for the 22 historic embroideries featured here.

At the same time *A Treasury of Embroidery Designs* takes the next logical step and presents adapted patterns and charts based upon these embroideries. We hope to encourage the reader to emulate the embroiderers of the past and to use their ideas and designs as a stepping stone to the creation of original embroideries.

This is not a radical idea. Since earliest times, ideas in art and design have crossed barriers of land, sea and language, with little respect for conventional frontiers. Embroidery, like any other form of art, has absorbed foreign influences and used them alongside familiar images as well as adapting them to meet current tastes and needs. Throughout our history, artists and designers have been inspired by a wealth of ideas and stimuli from literature, mythology, painting and theology, as well as other textile arts, and have readily transformed borrowed images into individual and original pieces of work.

A study of embroidery from any given period reveals the cultural trends of the day across the widest spectrum of society. Embroidery provides us with an intimate glimpse of the tastes and aspirations of the most privileged and the less fortunate. The application and use of embroidery has been equally wide: promoting images of majestic wealth and power of the state or church, adding an aura of grandeur to the lifestyle of the landed gentry or providing the means to decorate the simplest of costumes or the most humble of homes. Indeed the most prized embroideries owe their value not only to their rarity or place in history but more immediately to their unquestionable beauty, whatever the source may be.

The embroideries presented here, selected from museums and collections in Europe, Britain and the United States, demonstrate all these things, and above all the skill and superb technical achievements of past embroiderers.

Photographs alone cannot convey the special quality, the element of magic which radiates from the original embroidery itself. Visiting the collections represented here, and seeing in reality the embroideries featured has proved to be an impressive and exciting experience. It is this which has spurred us to adopt the methods of the past and to create embroideries inspired by these wonderful examples.

Each chapter in this book presents the reader with the opportunity to review or reflect upon a variety of influences and sources which bear relevance to a particular group of embroideries which share historical links or similarity of design. These embroideries are presented with working drawings and charts. Through sewing we have had the added pleasure of coming to a deeper appreciation of the expertise and brilliance of the embroiderers who were responsible for the original pieces. We hope that you will share the delight of the challenge that this brings and be tempted to experiment with some of the modified patterns in *A Treasury of Embroidery Designs*. We are indeed fortunate that so many historic embroideries are displayed in our museums and private collections and it is our hope that you will be further encouraged to discover for yourself the tremendous heritage that we possess.

STITCH GUIDE

The finished size of each embroidery, the stitches and materials used are given alongside the pattern. For all the uncharted patterns you will need to enlarge the drawings before you transfer them to the embroidery fabric. The easiest and most accurate way to enlarge a pattern is photographically. Most local instant print shops will be able to do this for you on a photocopying machine. The most effective method of tranferring this enlargement to the fabric is to use a well lit window as a light box. Stick the pattern to the window and place the embroidery fabric over it. You will then be able to trace the pattern on to the fabric. Alternately you can use dressmakers' carbon between the pattern and the fabric and press the design through. With either method make sure that the pencil or marker that you use can be removed from the fabric.

Diagrams for all the stitches used in this collection of embroideries follow, with a brief description of the working method.

underside, so that the needle appears a short distance ahead of the previous stitch. Re-insert the needle through the hole made by the previous stitch. Take care to make stitches small and even.

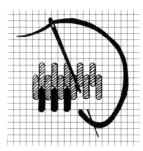

Brick Stitch
Worked from left to right over four threads of canvas leaving one stitch gap between each stitch. Subsequent rows are worked between these gaps.

Back Stitch
Work from right to left taking a small stitch backwards and then a large stitch on the

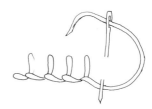

Open Buttonhole Stitch
Insert needle vertically towards the loops, covering the original thread with the needle. Keep the length of stitches and the space between them even.

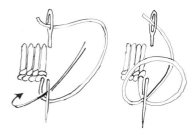

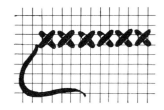

Tailor's Buttonhole Stitch
Work buttonhole stitch so that the knots lie close against each other. Make sure the thread is wrapped around the needle in the correct direction before pulling the needle through.

Cross Stitch
Cross stitch can be worked in two ways. Either complete each cross before working the next, or work all the diagonals in one direction before returning to work the diagonals in the other direction. For each method make sure that the top stitch is worked in the same direction each time.

Chain Stitch
Bring needle through fabric, loop thread under needle and hold with thumb, re-insert needle through hole it emerged from. Bring next stitch out a little ahead through most recent loop, taking care to pick up the same amount of fabric with each new stitch.

Long Armed Cross Stitch
The crossed stitches have one long arm and one short arm. Work from left to right completing each stitch before working the next.

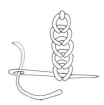

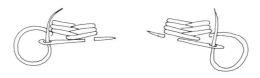

Broad Chain Stitch
Make first chain by passing the needle under a small running stitch. Insert needle into the same hole that it emerged from and take small stitch for next chain. Pass thread under loop of previous chain, and not through fabric.

Economy Stitch
Insert the needle a short space away from the right hand margin and bring it up at the edge. To return, the needle is inserted a small space from the left hand margin and up at its edge thus forming an overlapping stitch.

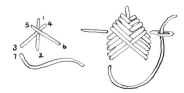

Fishbone Stitch

Start the stitch by emerging at 1 and follow the sequence of numbers, placing the next stitch just below 4. Keep the stitches close together to achieve a regular outline.

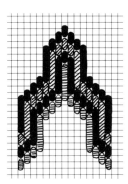

Hungarian Point

The stitch is worked in the same manner as florentine, but with stitches of two different lengths: one stitch over six threads and under one, followed by two or three stitches over two threads and under one, in zig zag rows.

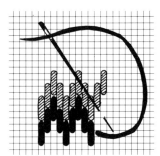

Florentine Stitch

Similar to brick stitch, but each stitch is worked over four threads and under two in zig zag lines.

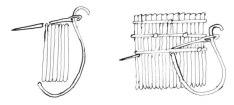

Laid and Couched Stitch

Work this stitch in two stages: firstly lay the initial threads evenly across the fabric, then lay the couching stitches at right angles to the first layer and couch down with tiny stitches at regular intervals on the return.

French Knots

Bring the needle up through the fabric and hold thread with left thumb. Twist the needle once round the thread and re-insert into the same hole, holding thread taut with left thumb for as long as possible in order to make a neat, tight stitch.

Long and Short Shading

The first row at the outer edge is worked with alternate long and short stitches. The subsequent rows are worked with stitches of even length which fit between the stitches of the previous row. The stitches should be packed close together for the best effect.

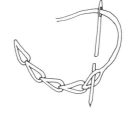

Outline Stitch

Work in the same way as STEM STITCH (see below), but keep the thread on the other side of the needle.

Split Stitch

The stitch is worked in the same way as STEM STITCH (see below) but the needle splits the thread as it emerges from a small backstitch.

Romanian Couching

Lay each thread across the fabric from left to right and couch it down with one central stitch on the return. This central stitch can be varied in length to achieve different textures.

Stem Stitch

Work this neat stitch from left to right by inserting the needle at regular intervals along the bottom line and bringing it through from the back at a slanting angle. Keep the thread to the same side of the needle throughout. The width of the stitch can be varied by changing the angle of the needle as it enters the fabric. Use stem stitch for outlines, or in close rows for STEM STITCH FILLING.

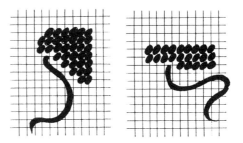

Encroaching Satin Stitch

Work the first row in SATIN STITCH (straight stiches closely worked to the required shape). On subsequent rows each stitch is placed between the stitch of the previous rows so that there is a slight overlap.

Tent Stitch

Tent stitch can be worked diagonally, which is best for filling large background areas, or horizontally.

In the diagonal method, the returning stitches fill in the gaps left by the previous row. For the horizontal method working from left to right, the needle is inserted from top to bottom so that there is overlap on the reverse. This gives a very firm and even stitch. To return, turn the work upside down and work in the same manner.

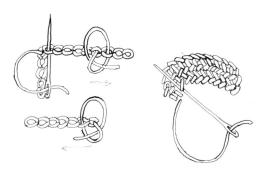

Trellis Stitch
Work small chain stitch around the area to be filled. This forms the basis of the first row of trellis stitch, and, since the trellis stitch is worked over the fabric and never through it, the chain stitches are used to anchor the finished work.

To form the first trellis stitch, take the needle up through the loop of a chain stitch and bring it back through the loop that its thread has formed. Pull the thread tight when it is almost all the way through to form the knot. Move to the next chain loop. On subsequent rows the trellis stitch is worked through the spaces between the previous row of knots. Trellis stitch is worked back and forth across the fabric.

To work the trellis stitch in a spiral, start in the centre with a small chain stitch. Fit as many trellis stitches into the loop of the chain stitch, and then continue to work through the spaces

between the knots as before, without changing direction. Catch down the finished filling to the outer edge with tiny stitches.

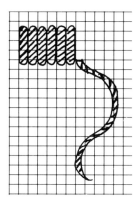

Upright Gobelin Stitch
The stitch is a canvas equivalent of satin stitch and can be worked over any number of canvas threads.

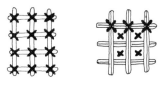

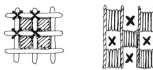

Fillings for Abigail Pett Bedcurtain (page 102)

1. Fragment of the Bayeux Tapestry (p 18).

2. Detail from a German church hanging (p 24).

3. Detail from the Holbein carpet (p 34).

4. 15th century German panel (p 29).

5. Long cushion cover from Chastleton House (p 40).

6. Cloud pattern hanging from Norway (p 44).

7. Blackwork pillowcover from the
Carew-Pole collection (p 53).

8. Late 16th century Blackwork panel (p 56)

9. Silk coverlet (p 59).

10. Tablecarpet depicting
the story of
Gombaut and Macée
(p 96).

11. Sampler from Vierlande (p 72).

12. 16th century panel from Hardwick Hall (p 75).

13. Detail from the
Marion Hanging,
Oxburgh Hall
(p 79).

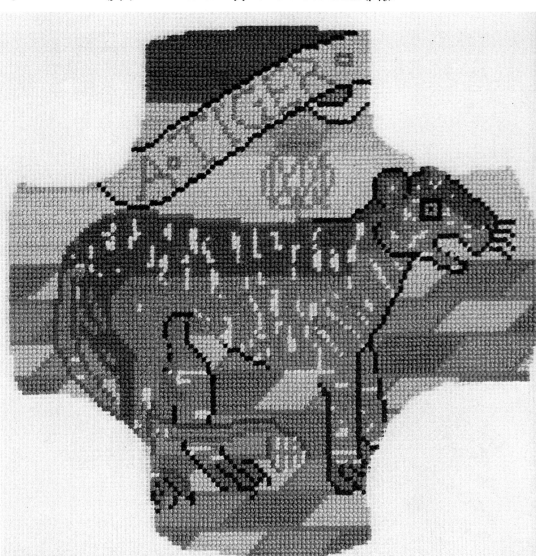

14. The Bradford Tablecarpet (p 91).

15. 17th century Dutch sampler (p 66).

16. 18th century American crewel coverlet (p 108).

7. 16th century embroidered panel from the Cooper-Hewitt Museum (p 86).

18. The Abigail Pett bed hangings (p 101).

19. Crewel coverlet from Littlecote House (p 105).

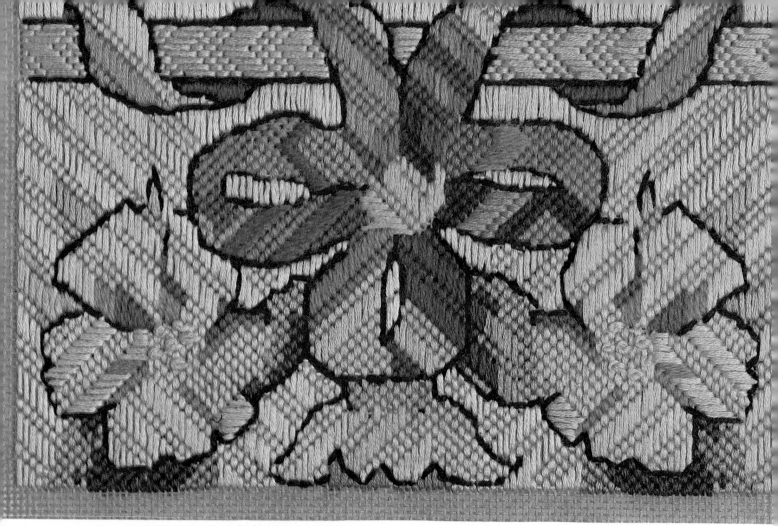

20. 17th century valance from the Cooper-Hewitt Museum (p 115).

21. Queen Anne Chair from Parham Park (p 118)

22. 19th century chasuble (p 123).

The Individual Projects

Bayeux Tapestry

Bayeux, France

For colour illustration of project see plate 1

It is our extraordinary good fortune that such a large and beautiful embroidery as the Bayeux Tapestry should have escaped the ravages of time to survive virtually intact for 900 years. The Bayeux Tapestry is the most complete example of embroidery in existence to display with such excellence the narrative style of the Romanesque period. There are many factors, other than rarity, which account for the special place that this embroidery has come to occupy. The historical accuracy of the events depicted, the fluency of the design or even the monumental scale on which it was worked would each alone have guaranteed this piece a place apart from all other embroideries. With such exceptional qualities, the Bayeux Tapestry serves as a basis upon which we can judge how the few surviving fragments of other medieval embroideries of this type may once have looked.

Bayeux Tapestry. The Latin inscription to this scene translates as: Here comes the messenger to Duke William.

The Bayeux Tapestry is in fact an embroidery. It was incorrectly classified as a tapestry many years ago, and the misnomer continues to this day as an eccentric English familiarity for a marvellous piece of embroidery which celebrates a special event in English history.

The design narrates, in seventy three consecutive scenes, a full, historic account of how William of Normandy conquered Harold Godwin of Wessex at the battle of Hastings in 1066. The images of the battle, of men and horses locked in combat, are so vividly portrayed that in the course of time it is these features which have made the embroidery world famous. However, the first thirty five scenes, almost half the embroidery, are devoted not to the battle but to the events which led William of Normandy to contest Harold's right to the English crown. The overall spirit of the piece does not, as one might expect, reflect the glory of war or victory, but implicitly illustrates the fate of Harold. Harold's demise is directly linked to his betrayal of a sacred oath of fidelity to William, taken on the holy relics at Bayeux Cathedral. This was an insult to the church of great magnitude and William's conquest gave him not only the English throne but also the satisfaction of exacting due punishment for such an outrageous and sacrilegious act.

The embroidery, relating all these facts and more, is approximately 20 inches deep and 230 feet long. Several lengths of the ground linen have been joined together to achieve this immense proportion. It is worked throughout in wool, in stem stitch and laid and couched work, a technique much favoured in Northern Europe throughout the Middle Ages. The style may seem at first to be rather naive, but it is in fact brilliantly conceived. The consummate skill and freshness of the drawings indicate that it was created by superb draughtsmen and embroiderers. There is no element present which is in any way superfluous and every part of the design is carefully planned to enable the story to flow unhindered. The large solid blocks of bright colour used for the horses and boats and the smaller splashes of colour in the buildings make no claim to naturalistic representation but are deftly used to enhance the overall effect and complement the lively drawing. The scenes are cleverly separated with trees spreading their branches to left and right, with buildings, or men turning away from the action to lead the eye into the next part of the tale. This prodigious embroidery not only delineates the conflict, but also gives a fund of information about the lives of people in the 11th century; the clothes they wore, the style of their architecture, their furniture and artifacts, the daily life of the peasants, their arms and armour. Together with the witty characterisation of the people, these add an element of humanity to a history of epic proportions.

To be able to generate such excitement in embroidery and to hold the viewer's attention so avidly is no mean achievement and it is clear that whoever was responsible for the design of the Bayeux Tapestry was well acquainted with the narrative form in art. There has been much discussion amongst scholars to determine where it was made. There is no conclusive evidence but it has been suggested, with authority, that the embroidery was commissioned by Odo, Bishop of Bayeux, half brother to William and, after the Battle of Hastings, also Bishop of Canterbury. The style of the drawing in the embroidery gives both Normandy and England an equal claim to be the place of origin, but since, at the time of its conception, Odo was closely connected with Canterbury it could be surmised that it was designed there. Canterbury was a renowned centre for the production of illustrated and illuminated manuscripts and although Norman manuscripts also reflect the English style of drawing, certain images in the embroidery have been recognised in manuscripts with a purely English pedigree. This again suggests that the design may come from Canterbury.

The designer, be he Norman or English, had a rich heritage and was able to call upon the vast repertoire of the medieval artist for his inspiration. Apart from the wealth of illuminated

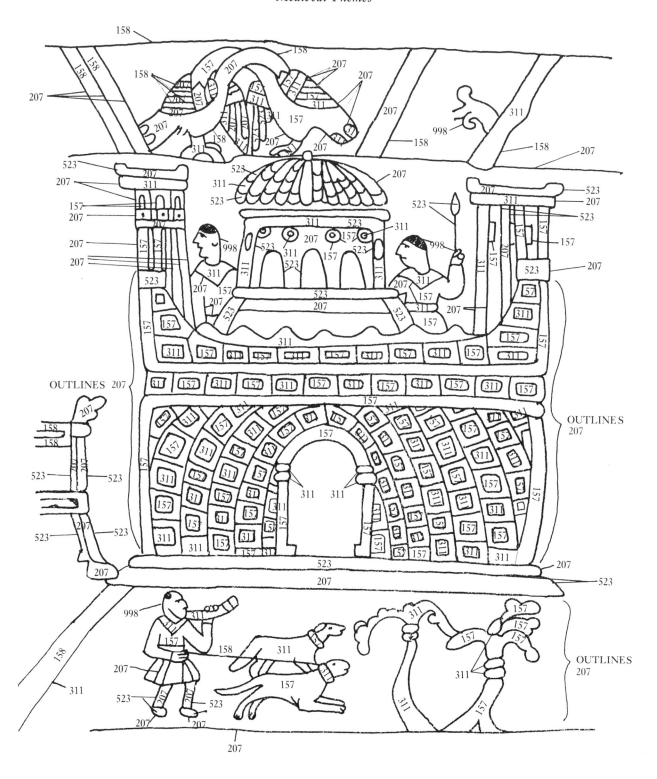

Bayeux Tapestry, fragment. Finished size: $12\frac{1}{2}'' \times 14''$.
Worked in laid and couched stitch for all solid areas, and
outline stitch for outlines, on chairback linen using
Appleton's single strand crewel wool.

Detail from a 13th century English manuscript. There were very close links between draughtsmanship and embroidery in the Middle Ages.

manuscripts with which he must have been familiar, birds and animals from Byzantine textiles and Celtic art, fables and allegories from current literature find their place within the decorative scheme of the embroidery.

The Bayeux Tapestry must have been conceived very soon after William's conquest. Certain events depicted are of such a personal nature that they would not have become a part of history had they not been noted here. In this way the embroidery has something of the character of modern reportage. General opinion is that it was designed and made between 1077 and 1082 when Bishop Odo fell from favour.

It has been suggested that the Bayeux Tapestry was used to decorate the nave of the cathedral at Bayeux during the feast of the relics. Hung down the length of the nave it would have formed a vast and magnificent decorative frieze. To the congregation of the Middle Ages this embroidery must have seemed like a vibrant and colourful morality play, reinforcing the mystical properties of the relics and the power of the church.

The Bayeux Tapestry, although it is the most extensive and complete embroidery of its type still in existence, was by no means unique in its time. The use of richly embroidered or woven hangings for decorating church interiors was common to most Northern European countries where the Romanesque architecture was relatively austere. These hangings can be viewed as an equivalent of the magnificent mosaic decorations found in the nave of San Vitale or Saint Peters at Ravenna, where glittering processions of Martyrs and Saints, or stories from the Bible emphasise how the narrative frieze style fitted into both the architecture and the spiritual ministry of the Christian church.

Northern Europe, with its long tradition of producing the finest ecclesiastical embroideries, looked to its own skills for the embellishment of churches rather than trying to emulate the mosaic work of the Byzantine church. The few fragments which survive belie the immense number of such embroideries which must have been made during the Middle Ages. The woven hangings and altar cloth from Halbestadt Cathedral, the altar cloths of Iceland, the Baldishol Tapestry and the embroidered frieze from Høyland church in Norway give us but a glimpse of former splendour.

That virtually every surviving item is ecclesiastical is not mere chance, but an illustration of just how the influence of the church had grown during the Middle Ages. The church provided a model of organisation and reasoned law in a fragmented Europe, and eventually came to dominate the many diverse kingdoms and unite them within a spiritual and pastoral network. The churches with their monasteries and attendant centres of learning enabled the Papacy to become the foremost patron of the Arts. Its influence could be felt everywhere and was continually strengthened by an international fraternity of monastic artisans, artists and scholars through whom ideas, skills and knowledge flowed from one country to another.

The fragment from an embroidered hanging from Høyland Church (below) dating from the end of the 12th century, shows a high degree of professionalism. It is possible that it was worked at the Convent at Niderholm rather than by a workshop or artisans from the wealthy, isolated, villages in the district of Høyland. Although it is a little later in date, very interesting comparisons can be made between this Norwegian embroidery and the Bayeux Tapestry. Even from this fragment it is clear that it was designated to fulfil the same function as an adornment of the church. The Høyland embroidery depicts the story of the Three Magi, and in the narrative style of Bayeux, shows them arriving in procession with their gifts. The Virgin and the infant Jesus stand within the framework of a building receiving their visitors from the East. The Star of Bethlehem shines out above the figures, bringing to mind a similar use of Halley's comet in the Bayeux Tapestry. The style of the drawing in the two embroideries is remarkably similar. The figures and the architectural features are treated in exactly the same way and the colours chosen by the embroiderers are from a similar palette – blue, yellow, red, green, black and white, with no pretence of naturalism.

It is in the execution and choice of stitches that the two embroideries differ. The Høyland piece is worked in outline stitch and refil stitch – a

Fragment from a late 12th century embroidered hanging from Høyland Church, which shares a narrative format with the Bayeux Tapestry.

running, darning stitch which closely resembles a woven surface. All the figurative elements are outlined in white linen thread with wool refil stitch creating the rich geometric patterns on the clothes of the Magi and the horse.

Refil stitch, or a stitch of a similar kind, was particularly popular in Scandinavia and Germany and was extensively used in Iceland, where it was known as 'glitsaumer' or 'skakkaglit', refil being their term for laid and couched work.

Church Hanging

Cloisters Museum, New York

For colour illustration of project see plate 2

This late 14th century German embroidery (opposite) in the Cloisters Museum in New York illustrates superbly many of the design elements and techniques found in embroideries and woven textiles of Northern Europe toward the end of the Medieval period. Worked in brick stitch with outline stitch, its characteristic geometric patterns echo the refil of the Høyland embroidery and the

darning stitch of the Icelandic altar cloth (below left). The barbed quatrefoil (below right) is used here to encase the different biblical scenes. It was a much favoured device for breaking up the ground of the designs, and was a marked feature of much Romanesque architecture. The figures holding inscribed banners reflect the tapestries woven at various workshops of the Low

Detail of late Medieval altar frontal from Iceland, using darning stitch.

Detail from a 15th century Icelandic hanging which uses the quatrefoil device.

24

Late 14th century German church hanging, now in the Cloisters Museum.

Countries at this time.

For its visual impact alone, the embroidery at the Cloisters would be considered of the highest calibre. Although it is no longer in its complete form (a further section of the embroidery once hung in a church in Westphalia but was lost in World War II and only a photograph now remains), it is in an almost perfect state of preservation. Each of the biblical scenes and the figures which form the lower and upper borders are a mass of geometric pattern. Created by the imaginative use of brick stitch, these are so varied and so ingeniously placed against each other that it is hard to believe that such a limited range of perhaps five or six colours was used to arrive at this dazzling feast of decorative texture.

25

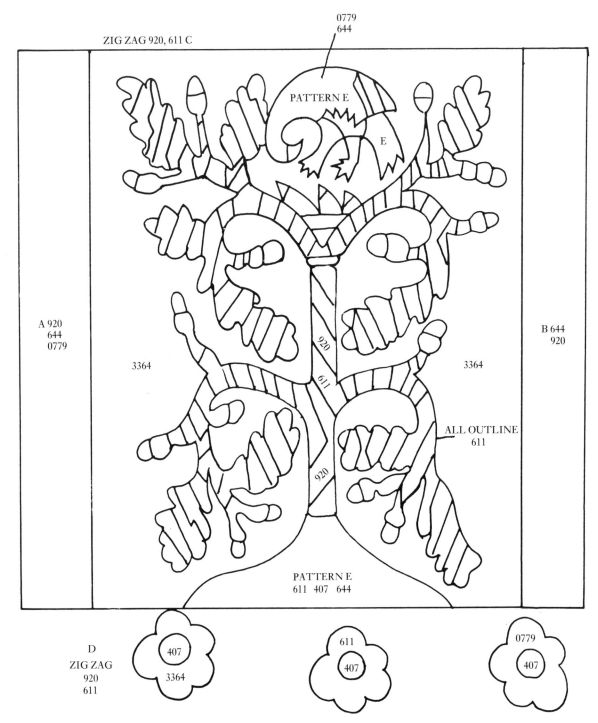

0779
644

ZIG ZAG 920, 611 C

PATTERN E

E

A 920
644
0779

B 644
920

3364

920

611

3364

ALL OUTLINE
611

920

PATTERN E
611 407 644

D
ZIG ZAG
920
611

407

3364

611

407

0779

407

ALL TREE STRIPED IN 920, 611
ALL BACKGROUND 3364

OPPOSITE PAGE

A AND B
PATTERN FOR SIDE BORDERS

C AND D
PATTERN FOR TOP BORDER AND BOTTOM BORDER.
WORK THREE ROWS OF EACH COLOUR

E
OUTLINE OF PATTERN FOR THE BASE OF THE TREE.
WORK IN 611. FILLING STITCHES ARE WORKED IN 407
AND 644
USE THE SAME OUTLINE PATTERN FOR THE BODY
AND TAIL OF THE BIRD USING 0779 AND FILLING
WITH 644

F
HOW THE STITCHES FALL IN THE TRUNK OF THE
TREE

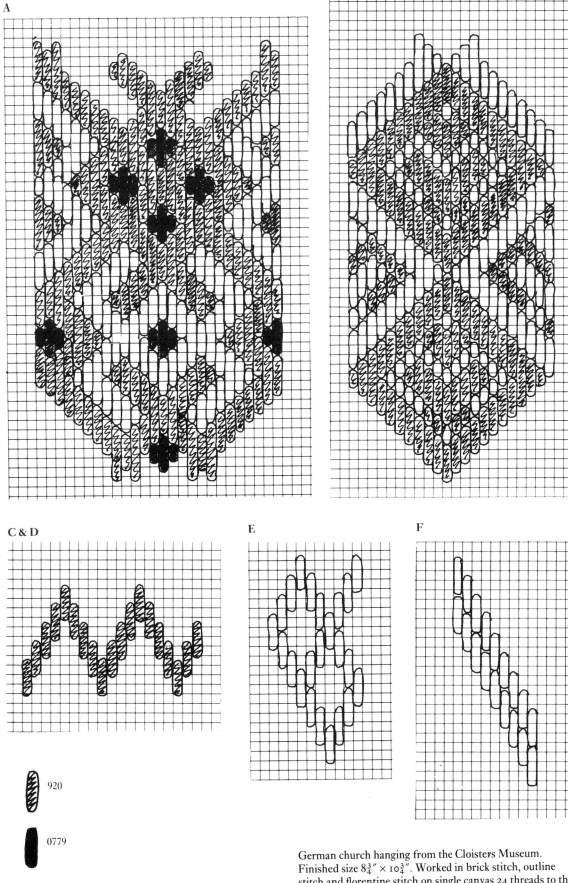

A

B

C & D

E

F

920

0779

644

German church hanging from the Cloisters Museum. Finished size $8\frac{3}{4}'' \times 10\frac{3}{4}''$. Worked in brick stitch, outline stitch and florentine stitch on single canvas 24 threads to the inch, with Anchor and DMC stranded embroidery cotton. 6 strands for brick stitch and florentine stitch and 2 strands for outline stitch.

From the 12th century to the 14th century a type of English embroidery, known universally as Opus Anglicanum, was the most sought after and treasured by all the great religious centres. Elaborate copes and chasubles, finely embroidered in gold, silver and coloured silks, often with the further enrichment of precious jewels, were worked in England by embroiderers whose skill was unrivalled throughout Europe.

While Opus Anglicanum was the product of highly organised, professional workshops, evidence has shown that, in Germany, important embroideries were often carried out by the contents attached to the great cathedrals. Centres for the production of church embroideries grew up in Hildesheim, Luneburg and Weisenheim, where the abbesses would overlook the work carried out by the younger nuns. In the middle Ages, convents were not only places for contemplative retreat but also the refuge of nobly-born unmarried women. Unable, for reasons of rank, to consider other forms of occupation, they lived and worked side by side with their vocational sisters. As a result, a certain secularism and worldliness began to creep into their work, lending it a characteristic charm.

The style of the Cloisters embroidery would suggest that it was the product of such a convent. Certain elements of the design – the acorns, leaves and birds in the borders, and the two-dimensional treatment of figures – have led researchers to believe that it is from the Lower Saxony area of Germany. The embroidery came to the Cloisters from the Hohenzollen-Sigmaringen Collection where, in 1874, it was attributed to any one of the religious houses attached to the medieval diocese of Hildesheim.

While continuing the tradition of using church embroideries as a means of religious instruction as well as adornment, the Cloisters hanging illustrates the symbolic interpretations of the Bible which were under constant review by theologians during the Middle Ages. One of their main preoccupations was to establish a structured, predetermined relationship between events in the Old and New Testaments. Vast commentaries were amassed which went to great lengths to list as many symbolic connections as could possibly be found. By the early 14th century this thesis of 'prefiguration' had grown to such enormous proportions and had become so complicated and obscure that the time was ripe for simplification. The *Speculum Humanae Salvationis* was written with the express purpose of clarifying the theme so that it could be understood by less brilliant minds and be used for the instruction of a wider audience. The straight-forward approach of the *Speculum*, using pictures with short explanatory notes, was highly successful and it proved to be an invaluable aid to teaching theological thought as well as an inexhaustible source of design concepts for artists and embroiderers alike.

Sections from a set of 15th century tapestries in the Metropolitan Museum in New York are a splendid example of how the theme of prefiguration was incorporated into the decorative scheme of church hangings. This set depicts the seven sacraments of Baptism, Confirmation and Tonsure, Holy Eucharist, Penance, Marriage and Extreme Unction together with their prefigurations from the Old Testament – Adam and Eve with God the Father being the prefiguration of Marriage; Jacob blessing his children that of Confirmation etc.

The biblical scenes depicted in the Cloisters embroidery expound the treatise of prefiguration in a visually dynamic and exciting way, and it is likely that the *Speculum* or certain other writings of a similar nature were used as a source.

15th Century Panel

Museum für Kunst und Gewerbe, Hamburg

For colour illustration of project see plate 4

Medieval philosophers were greatly attracted to the mysterious, the mythical and the symbolic in their search for a better understanding of the world. The works of the classical scholars were as important to them as they are to us today. Pre-Christian thought was interpreted and adapted until it was compatible with the ideals of Christianity.

The existence of the mysterious and elusive unicorn was first recorded by a Greek writer as early as 400 BC and from then on it held a curious attraction. The unicorn was claimed to have been seen in India by travellers who described him variously as horse-like, stag-like, with the body of a goat and with cloven hooves. He ascribed the attributes of immense physical power and courage, a beast who chose to die at the hands of the hunter rather than to submit and be taken captive. Even the earliest description of the unicorn alludes to his magical powers and clearly states that drinking vessels made from his horn would render harmless any poisons and prevent convulsions and falling sickness. It was not long before the unicorn himself became the symbol of purity. The Greek and Roman philosophers, greatly revered in the Middle Ages, substantiated the existence of the unicorn, though none claimed to have actually seen one.

Eventually a legend grew up around this fabulous beast which exactly fitted his elusive nature. This told how the unicorn, the most fearless and awesome of beasts, who was hunted for the magical properties of his horn, fought steadfastly and ferociously against capture and continually evaded the hunters and their dogs. Unable to take him by force the hunstmen resorted to cunning and lured the unicorn into the presence of a virgin maid, for the one weakness of the unicorn was his inability to resist the attraction of chastity. Once he had been tamed into submission by the maid, the hunters could make their move and ensnare him with ease.

It is curious and surprising to find the early theologians of the Christian church adopting the legend of the unicorn to symbolise the life of Christ and the divine plan for the redemption of mankind. Anomalies such as the unsuitability of the maid, with her dishonest role, to be a symbol for the Virgin Mary or the unicorn's overtly sexual nature in pagan mythology, presented no problems to the theologians, who cited the many biblical references to the unicorn to rectify any inconsistencies. Saint Ambrose, Bishop of Milan, wrote in his commentary of the Psalms, 'who then is this unicorn but the only begotten son of God'.

Thus the pagan myth was transformed and the unicorn became a substantial part of the rich symbolism of the early Christian church. The universal acceptance of the existence of the unicorn was further strengthened by his inclusion in the writing of Physiologus (the scientist). His text consisted of descriptions of animals, birds and fishes and fanciful descriptions of mythological or imagined creatures, such as the autolops, caladruis, unicorn and upopa. Each

Right: detail from 15th century panel in Hamburg. Finished size $9\frac{1}{2}'' \times 10\frac{3}{4}''$. Stitches used: satin stitch for all berries, diagonal stalks and animal horns, brick stitch for big leaves and vertical stalks, mixture of brick stitch and long and short stitch for animal body, all worked with 6 strands of DMC or Anchor Stranded Embroidery Cotton. For the outline (tiny back stitch) use only 3 strands of embroidery cotton.

COLOUR KEY

A 3011 DMC
B 3051 DMC
C 0862 ANCHOR
D 612 DMC
E 3052 DMC
F 0281 ANCHOR
G 0860 ANCHOR
H 0831 ANCHOR
BLACK OUTLINE

Opposite: 15th century German panel.

Late 15th century tapestry, from the Burrell Collection, 'The Persuite of Fidelity',
which makes use of the popular allegory of the hunt.

account concluded with lessons to be learnt by Christians from the supposed habits and characteristics of the animals described. The Physiologus was so admired and enjoyed in the Middle Ages that many translations were made of it, making it available to a public from places as far apart as the Middle East and Iceland. As time went on, revised editions were compiled and many creatures were added to the original text. By the 12th century these enlarged versions were

generally known in Western Europe as bestiaries.

The unicorn story was taken up in the 12th century by poets and writers of romantic tales as a symbol of the lover beguiled by his beloved. The juxtaposition of secular and religious symbolism was not uncommon in the Middle Ages – the God of earthly love and the God of Heaven were not incompatible.

With such a wealth of pagan and Christian lore at their disposal, the artists of the Middle Ages had rich sources to draw upon for their designs and it is not surprising that they used them so well. The 14th and 15th centuries saw the weaving of the most beautiful tapestries in which mythical and real creatures from the bestiaries played their symbolic part. A set of five superb small tapestries in the Metropolitan Museum, New York, uses the story of the stag hunt as an allegory of life, whilst a tapestry in the Burrell Collection, Glasgow, known as 'The Pursuit of Fidelity, (opposite) shows 'fidelity' in the form of a stag being chased by two lovers on horseback, accompanied by their dogs.

Perhaps the most famous tapestries to depict the hunt of the unicorn are those now hanging in the Cloisters Museum. Without any symbolic overtones these tapestries would be considered of great importance for their beauty of colour, their exquisite delineation and the sheer magnitude of their conception. However, beyond this, they reveal all the symbolic interpretations the Christian church could offer on the subject of the hunt and capture of this most fabulous of beasts.

The embroidery from the Museum für Kunst und Gewerbe, Hamburg, (photograph on page 30) is on a much smaller and more approachable scale than the vast tapestries at the Cloisters but this piece has importance too, for it illustrates in its own simple and unostentatious way how the story of the unicorn filtered into all manner of embroideries and decorative textiles. The Hamburg embroidery, with its primitive drawing and gentle charm, uses the imagery of the unicorn and the virgin maid together with a hunter and his dog, and dragons and stags, in a repeating pattern of coiling vines laden with fruit. Originating, it is thought, from a convent in the region of Luneburg, Germany in the 15th century, this pieces displays both Christian and pre-Christian symbolism of purity, fidelity and fruitfulness side by side in perfect harmony. It is possibly that this embroidery is a fragment of a larger piece, perhaps designed to hang in the choir or decorate the altar of a church on festival days.

Holbein Carpet (fragment)

Victoria and Albert Museum, London

For colour illustration of project see plate 3

In the early 16th century, England's transition out of the Middle Ages and into the era of the Renaissance is marked by the unquestionable brilliance, sensitivity and skill of one artist, Holbein. Hans Holbein first came to England in 1526, having already, at the early age of 28, established for himself a fine reputation in Europe as an artist of considerable merit.

He was born in Germany, but his family moved to Basle, in Switzerland, in 1514 and it is the cultural trends he encountered in Basle, during his formative years, which underlie Holbein's subsequent development as an artist. Basle was then the established centre for the new medium of printing and the print workshops attracted some of the great philosophers, humanists and artists to their sides. It is known that Holbein produced a considerable quantity of designs and illustrations for engravers and in particular for the master printer Johannes Froben. It was at the Froben print workshop that Holbein came into contact with this highly cultured milieu and most importantly with the most renowned humanist of the age, Erasmus, for whom Holbein illustrated *In Praise of Folly*. Erasmus made a profound impression on Holbein and it was at his request that Holbein made his first visit to England to paint a portrait of Sir Thomas More, Lord High Chancellor of England.

This was the time of the Reformation when England, along with the rest of Europe during the late 15th century and the early 16th, was going through a period of transition. The monarchy in England was stronger than at any previous time. Henry VII, founder of the Tudor dynasty, was able to pass on to his son Henry VIII a united realm which he ruled as an autocrat. The old medieval order, with its political and religious domination by the Papal Church, was being questioned, as the papacy was no longer seen to be fulfilling its role of spiritual leadership. The Pope was considered by many to be no more than a remote Italian prince, draining Europe of her rescources (through indulgences and dispensations), to support extravagance and corruption. The excesses of the monasteries, where religious fervour had waned, and where lax attitudes and the overt relish for wealth and comfort had become commonplace, only served to strengthen growing concern. Throughout Europe, articulate and literate humanists sought to bring about change from within the church. Their failure to achieve any reform or to stay further degeneration ultimately led to the irreversible, ideological split between the Church of Rome and the new Protestantism. Under pressure from the advance of the ideals of the Reformation, the Catholic Church withdrew from being the major patron of the arts.

Henry VIII's desire to divorce his wife, Catherine of Aragon, against the decree of the Pope and the Catholic Church was the spur needed for England to become, in 1534, the first country to subordinate the power of the church to that of the crown. Henry VIII was skilfully

16th century embroidered Holbein carpet, fragment.

guided by Thomas Cromwell throughout the negotiations which resulted in the severance from Rome and brought the Reformation to England. Henry's subsequent position as head of the Church of England, embodying the church, state and law, gave him a unique advantage – he proclaimed himself answerable to no-one but God. The dissolution of the monasteries, urged by Thomas Cromwell, released funds for Henry to lavish wheresoever he wished. As a 'Renaissance Prince' he sought the very best from the civilized world and sent emissaries to Italy, Flanders and France for masters of every art, in order that his court might surpass all in splendour. He vied with other monarchs of Europe to have the finest collection of paintings, tapestries and furnishings. The court of Henry VIII grew to be a spectacular manifestation of wealth, power and learning.

It was against this background and during the time he spent in England, that Holbein reached his true eminence as a painter, draughtsman and designer and pioneered the development of secular art patronised by the state rather than by the church. He was elevated into the Tudor Court by Thomas Cromwell and became known as the 'King's Painter'. Holbein was a true Renaissance man; remarkably innovative and able to turn his inestimable talents to any field of design. He designed jewellery, stained glass, dagger sheaths, plate and architectural details; made wood engravings and worked on murals. However, it is for his superbly perceptive portraits that he is justly most famous. The paintings are rich in decorative detail, yet have a quiet clarity and dignity. His concern to reveal and record the very fabric of the society he chose to adopt is reflected in his acute observation not only of his subject but also of the objects and fashionable trappings which surround the individual portrayed. The most favoured accessories, which appear time and time again, are the wonderful knotted carpets of the Orient.

The carpets first appear in his series of portraits of the wealthy Hanseatic merchants based in London. This fraternity of the Hansa

League exercised considerable control of most of Europe's import and export trade. Hamburg, Lubeck, Novgorod, London, Bergen and Bruges were all towns linked within the Hansa trading network. Furs from Russia, wood and fish from Norway would be traded for English wool and manufactured goods or Italian silks and gold. Certainly oriental carpets would have been included in the list of commodities traded between the nations. Because they were so rare and so expensive, these carpets were regarded as a status symbol denoting the wealth and prestige of the owner, and eventually, it would seem that no portrait by Holbein was complete without a patch of eastern carpet appearing in it somewhere.

Eastern carpets were well known in Moorish Spain long before they were introduced to the rest of Europe. Records of the marriage of Eleanor of Castille to Edward I of England in 1255, mention her bringing with her these wonderful textiles. At the wedding festivities, Spanish and Oriental carpets lined the streets and hung from the walls of the Spanish Ambassador's house in celebration. However, the importation of carpets from the East on a commercial basis was not until much later and whilst Spain may have been the original supplier, the great mercantile cities of Italy, who carried on a lively trade with Turkey, could well have been responsible for the limited supply of these rare carpets to Western Europe. Indeed, the visual history of the carpet in the West can be traced through its representation in Italian paintings from the early 14th century onwards. The carpets were portrayed so accurately that various pattern groups have been given an artist's name to distinguish them from others. Hence the Bellini carpet, the Lotto carpet, the Crivelli carpet, and later (as carpets appeared in the paintings of Northern Europe), the Memling carpet, the large pattern Holbein and the small pattern Holbein carpet.

Even by Holbein's time, eastern carpets were still a rare and costly item and those fortunate enough to possess them used their carpets with

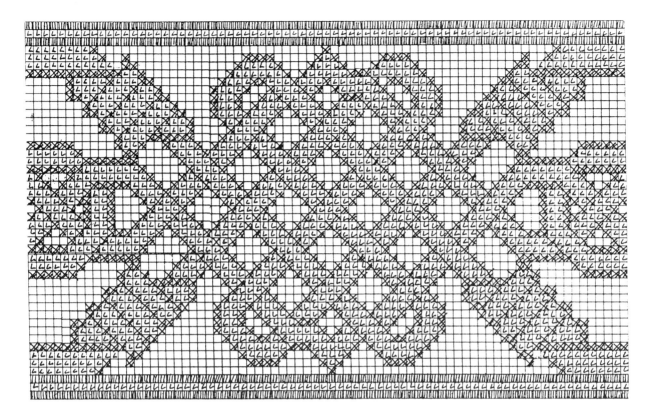

Holbein carpet, fragment. Finished size 8½″ × 5½″. Worked in Appleton's tapestry wool on linen double canvas. 9 holes to the inch.

COLOUR KEY

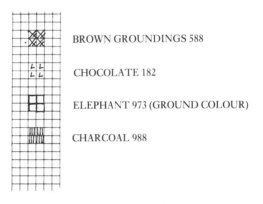

BROWN GROUNDINGS 588

CHOCOLATE 182

ELEPHANT 973 (GROUND COLOUR)

CHARCOAL 988

great care. They were seldom, if ever, used on the floor, rather they were draped over tables or used as cupboard covers, adding rich colour and texture to the austere oak furniture. It is interesting that paintings of Henry VIII invariably show him standing squarely on a beautiful eastern carpet – what better way to advertise his supreme power and wealth?

The technique of making knotted carpets was quite unknown outside the East and Spain (where Mudejars, Muslems living within Christian Spain copied eastern models) and therefore England and several other European countries began to produce embroidered carpets to emulate the original knotted ones and to supplement imports. Although initially these embroidered carpets were conceived purely as copies, they soon began to achieve a highly individual style of their own.

The new and beautiful patterns from the East became simplified and were blended with the indigenous northern style. The carpet presented a new and exciting format which allowed for both the direct absorption of foreign design influences and for a renewed harmony with our own Celtic culture. The design of the small pattern Holbein carpet, with its repeating pattern of angular

37

16th century embroidered tablecarpet from the Landesmuseum, Zurich.

interlaced octagons and cross shaped arabesques was readily adaptable to the embroidered technique.

The fragment of an embroidered Holbein carpet from the collection at the Victoria and Albert Museum (see page 35), shows this remarkably well and also demonstrates the coming together of East and West. The interlaced octagons are clearly derived from the original eastern designs but the borders, which on the imported carpets would have utilised a form of Kufic script, have here become transformed into the rhythmic flowing lines of interlacing and endless knots. The spirit of the magnificent 'carpet' pages to be found in the Lindisfarne Gospels and the Book of Durrow (right) harmonises here with the spirit of Islam.

Holbein's fine depiction of carpets in his portraits would be reason enough for his name to be attached to certain designs, but his known connection with a wide variety of decorative arts leads one to make further suppositions about his interest in carpets, particularly the embroidered ones. During Holbein's lifetime the guilds of the broderers, goldsmiths and wyre drawers in England were very closely connected, for all were dependent on gold and silver for their trade (the broderers having a need for a steady supply of gold and silver thread). Holbein is known to have designed gold plate, chains and jewellery for Henry VIII and would naturally have had dealings with the guilds. It would not be unreasonable to speculate that Holbein, with his unique range of talents and his obvious love of the rare Caucasian carpets, would have been tempted to produce patterns for the broderers to copy. It was not unusual at this time for artists to step over the boundaries of their own fields to use their expertise in other areas of design. It is interesting to note that the 'Holbein' style of embroidered carpet was also produced in Switzerland during the 16th century, which further reinforces the connection between Holbein and these designs.

Detail from the Carpet Page of the Book of Durrow (Trinity College Library, Dublin). Carpet pages made extensive use of knotted patterns.

The embroidered carpet from the Landesmuseum, Zurich (opposite page), is a lovely example of the type of embroidered carpet being produced in Switzerland during the 16th century. This piece, dated 1533, is relatively early in the history of embroidered carpets and again demonstrates how well the eastern design elements were assimilated into the embroidered technique. In the borders only small elements of Kufic script remain in an otherwise purely northern treatment.

Long Cushion Cover

Chastleton House, Oxfordshire

For colour illustration of project see plate 5

Imports of fabulous silks, velvets and brocades from Italy made a profound impact on English design. The individual elements were not as foreign as one might suppose for the Moorish or Mediterranean influence was already to be found in English embroidery, reflecting the earlier Spanish taste brought to the Royal Tudor court by Catherine of Aragon. However, the new imports presented exciting variations on familiar designs. The arabesque and diaper patterns were quickly taken up by embroiderers who put their considerable skill to the production of glorious clothes and furnishings of a secular nature. The introduction and widespread acceptance of the pomegranate motif to English designers and embroiderers must be directly attributed to Catherine, as it was her personal device. Such was the esteem in which she was held by the English nation that the pomegranate's association with her promoted its continued use in all manner of design, especially textiles and embroidery, until long after her death.

The pomegranate motif has ancient roots and can be traced in one form or another back to the relief stonework of the Assyrian Palace of Assurnasirpal, 883–859 BC, where it was shown growing in the tree of life, symbolising fertility. The Sassanian silks of the 4th century AD which were the inspiration for many Byzantine textile designs, also show the pomegranate image.

The 16th century long cushion cover from Chastleton House.

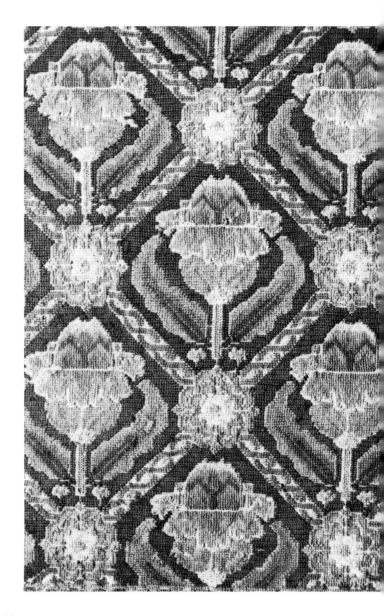

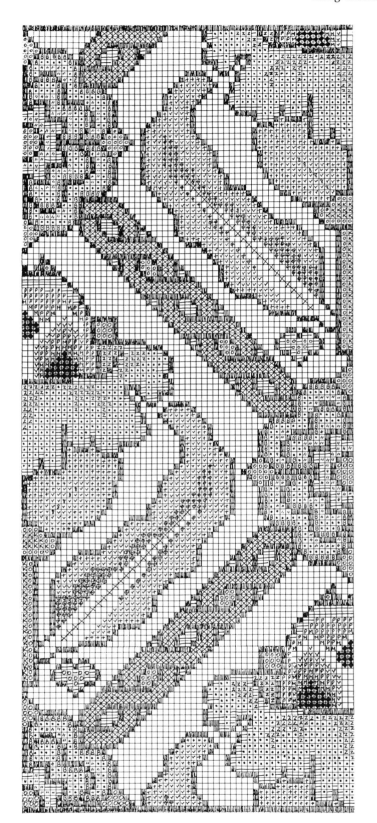

Long cushion cover from Chastleton House. Worked in cross stitch on 14 hole double canvas using 2 strands crewel wool and 6 strands embroidery cotton. Approximate size 8″ × 10″. Pattern repeat size 8″ × 8″.

COLOUR KEY

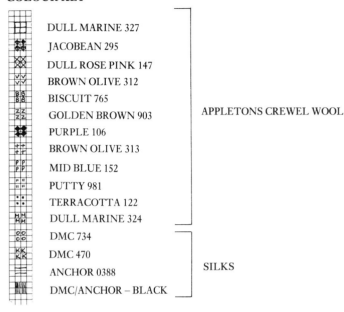

	DULL MARINE 327
	JACOBEAN 295
	DULL ROSE PINK 147
	BROWN OLIVE 312
	BISCUIT 765
	GOLDEN BROWN 903
	PURPLE 106
	BROWN OLIVE 313
	MID BLUE 152
	PUTTY 981
	TERRACOTTA 122
	DULL MARINE 324

APPLETONS CREWEL WOOL

	DMC 734
	DMC 470
	ANCHOR 0388
	DMC/ANCHOR – BLACK

SILKS

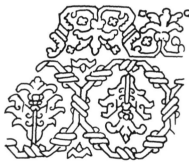

Pomegranate image found on a 16th century Italian sampler in the Victoria and Albert Museum.

A lovely example of how the pomegranate was used in 16th century English embroidery can be seen at Chastleton House, Oxfordshire. Here a long cushion cover (opposite page) features this exotic bloom set within a repeating diaper framework of twisted bands of colour, fashioned 'barley sugar' style. The overall design of the cushion is very derivative of the Italian silk brocades, but the inclusion of a Tudor rose at each barley sugar intersection stamps upon it a very English character. The colours have now

16th century English embroidered tablecarpet now at the Art Institute of Chicago, which has similar pomegranate and 'barley sugar' motifs to the Chastleton long cushion.

Outline chart for the full embroidery.

Chastleton House is set within the heart of what was once one of England's main wool producing areas. England's economy from the Middle Ages until the Industrial Revolution was based on the trade of wool. Walter Jones, owner and builder of Chastleton, made his fortune as a merchant supplying wool to local trades and craftsmen, and more importantly direct to the Italian textile industry. It is not surprising to find Italian influences represented amongst the furnishings of his home. The long cusion is now displayed in the middle chamber of Chastleton House. In this room the pomegranate motif is also to be found employed in a handsome plasterwork frieze.

A further development of the pomegranate image forms the design of the ground of an English 16th century embroidered tablecarpet at the Chicago Institute of Art (opposite page). This exceptionally fine piece presents no fewer than eight variations of the pomegranate motif worked in a combination of rich glowing colours. Each pomegranate is a wonderfully intricate form and, as in the case of the Chastleton long cushion, is set within a 'barley sugar' framework. The beauty of this unique tablecarpet is further enhanced by the borders composed of a series of twelve vignettes depicting episodes from the Bible. These scenes have been directly linked to the engravings of Gerarde de Jode and to the work of Martin de Voss.

faded and are quiet and subdued, but a glimpse of the reverse reveals all the bright original hues, so loved by the 16th century embroiderers.

Wall Hanging

Norsk Folkemuseum, Bygdøy, Norway

For colour illustration of project see plate 6

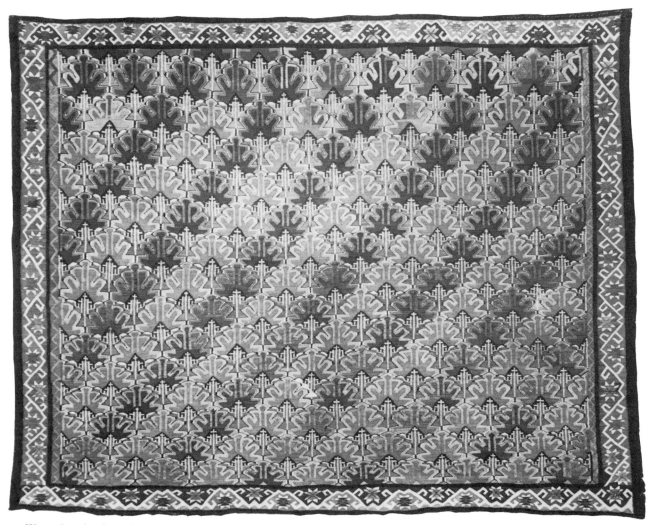

Woven hanging from the Norsk Folkemuseum, featuring the cloud pattern.

It is not known when the pomegranate image was first introduced to Norway, but evidence suggests that the use of the motif is very old indeed. The sagas tell of the Viking traders who returned to Norway from Byzantium with magnificent clothes made from silks, and it would not be unreasonable to surmise that the pomegranate motif, a most favoured design element of Byzantine textiles, could have been included amongst those silks. The marriage of Don Philipus of Castile to Kristina, daughter of King Haakon 4th, in Bergen, Norway in 1258 gives further emphasis to the early knowledge and contact which existed between Scandinavian and Mediterranean cultures. However, it was not until the 16th century that the flow of imported goods (including Italian textiles brought into Bergen by the Hanseatic merchants) reintroduced the pomegranate motif and created a revival of interest in its design possibilities.

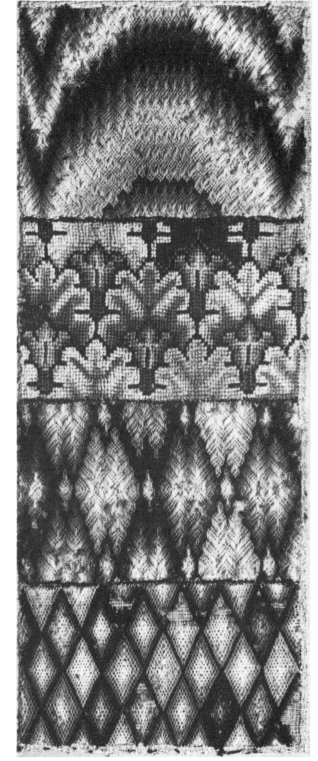

Moroccan mosque decoration, Bo Inania Fez.

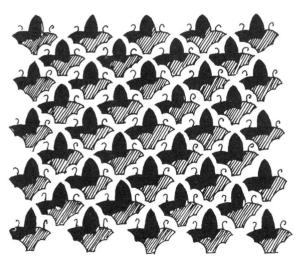

18th century German sampler from the Bayerisches Museum in Munich.

From the few surviving Norwegian tapestries of the early 17th century, which mark its reintroduction, one can trace how the pomegranate motif was gradually adapted to the limitations of their weaving technique. By the 18th century it had been refined into a stylised image, much less flower-like and more akin to a palmette. In this form, the design known as Skybragdmønster (the cloud pattern) was assimilated into the traditional stock of designs which appear repeatedly in Norwegian woven hangings. Curiously, what would seem to be a radical change in the image in fact draws it full circle and echoes the very earliest form of the pomegranate motif in Europe, in the architectural details on the Alhambra and in Cordoba, and the mosques of Morocco (page 45, left).

The cloud pattern was used on countless large woven hangings, cushion covers and long bench covers continually until the 19th century. The tapestry featured on the wall hanging from the Textile Collection at the Folkmuseum, Bygdøy, Norway (page 44) is believed to have been produced in the district of Vågå, Gudbrandsdal, an area renowned throughout Scandinavia for the production of the finest of all peasant woven hangings. This example, which displays so well the handsome cloud pattern woven to form a wallhanging or wall carpet, has a patterned border very reminiscent of eastern carpet designs. The influence of the oriental carpet designs had clearly reached this far into Northern Europe. No doubt the versatility of the cloud pattern, which adapted easily from the very largest to the smallest scale of tapestry, was in some measure the reason why it stayed such a firm favourite for over 300 years.

The German development of the pomegranate makes an interesting comparison with the woven tapestries of Norway. The refinement and transformation into the palmette/cloud pattern is virtually uniform, but in Germany it was almost always embroidered, usually in cross stitch. An enormous quantity of samplers, worked in wool on canvas were produced in Germany during the 18th and 19th centuries (illustration on page 45, right shows one example). The Bayerisches Museum in Munich has a very comprehensive collection displaying the amazing similarity of these samplers which called upon a relatively small range of geometric patterns. Amongst the repeating motifs and florentine designs, one invariably finds a small area of cloud pattern, underlining its great popularity and the versatility which allowed it to be worked both in embroidery and in woven textiles.

Opposite and following pages: wallhanging chart from the Norsk Folkemuseum. Approximate size $7\frac{1}{2}'' \times 10''$. Worked in tent stitch on 16 gauge canvas using 2 strands of Appleton's crewel wool.

Chart A

Chart B

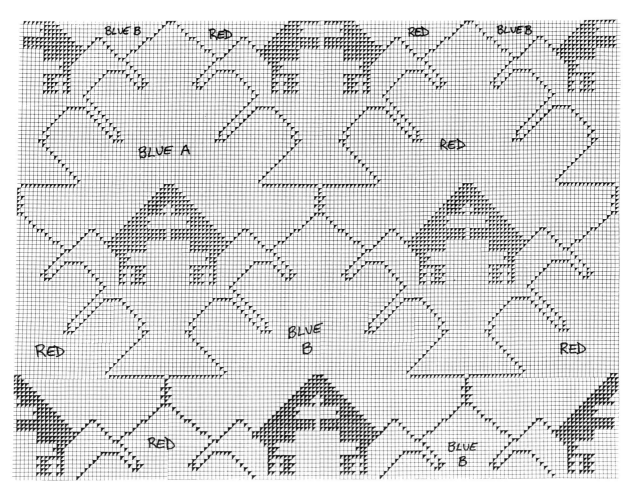

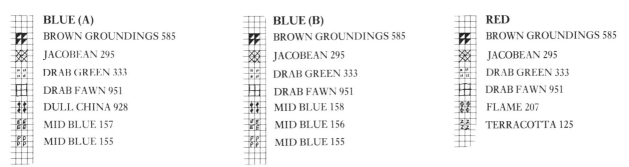

Outline chart for the full embroidery.

COLOUR KEY

BLUE (A)

	BROWN GROUNDINGS 585
	JACOBEAN 295
	DRAB GREEN 333
	DRAB FAWN 951
	DULL CHINA 928
	MID BLUE 157
	MID BLUE 155

BLUE (B)

	BROWN GROUNDINGS 585
	JACOBEAN 295
	DRAB GREEN 333
	DRAB FAWN 951
	MID BLUE 158
	MID BLUE 156
	MID BLUE 155

RED

	BROWN GROUNDINGS 585
	JACOBEAN 295
	DRAB GREEN 333
	DRAB FAWN 951
	FLAME 207
	TERRACOTTA 125

3 ELIZABETHAN

Blackwork is monochrome embroidery and, as its name implies, was most often worked in black silk on a white or natural linen ground. It has distinctive characteristics giving it its own separate place in the embroidery of the 15th, 16th and 17th centuries.

The patterns which are an integral part of most types of Blackwork have their roots in the Middle East. The interlacing and tiny geometric forms found in early examples of this type of embroidery clearly stem from the culture of Moslem countries where figurative design is discouraged by the teachings of the Koran. It is generally considered that Blackwork was introduced into Europe primarily through Spain. Under the domination of the Moors until 1472, Spain had been subject to Moorish influences for seven centuries. Interlacing quatrofoils, stars, lozenges and arabesques, showing the Islamic principles of non-figurative symmetry were seen in all types of Spanish decorative art.

Although it was not until the 16th century that Blackwork became a prominent part of English domestic embroidery, it featured as a decorative element at a much earlier date. Chaucer, writing at the end of the 14th century describes the dress of a young wife in the Miller's Tale:

> *Her smock was white, embroidery repeated*
> *Its pattern on the collar front and back*
> *Inside and out, it was of silk and black*
> *And all the ribbons of her milky mutch*
> *Were made to match her collar, even such*

Portraits showing small-scale geometric embroidery decorating collars and cuffs indicate that by the early 1500s Blackwork was already an established feature of fashionable dress. So precise was Holbein's exquisite rendering of Blackwork in many of his portraits that the double running stitch used in the execution of the embroidery became known as 'Holbein stitch'.

This much favoured style of Blackwork embroidery, holding firmly to the Moorish-influenced geometric patterns, continued in Europe and these popular designs eventually became absorbed into the folk culture of both eastern and western Europe. On the Island of Marken in North Holland, cross stitch embroidery worked exclusively in black silk on white linen is an integral part of the national costume. The patterns based on the geometric zig-zag, stars and stylised floral forms are used to decorate neckbands, apron string tabs, chin straps and ribbons.

In the 13th century a Spanish King was married in Haakonshallen, Bergen, to a Norwegian princess and the direct contact and influence of Moorish Spain is still to be seen as part of the national costume in a few districts on the west coast of Norway. For example, in the district of Voss, starlike motifs worked in black silk in cross stitch and Holbein stitch are found on the traditional linen headgear, reflecting the close contact there must once have been between these two countries (opposite). In other countries the black has been substituted by other colours

Patterns taken from a Norwegian headscarf,
from the Historisk Museum, Bergen.

but the roots of the design are clear, and they
remain in the repertoire of traditional
embroideries from the Mediterranean to the
North Sea. In England during the 16th and 17th
centuries Blackwork embroidery developed away
from purely geometric patterns to include all the
characteristics of the Elizabethan age.

Domestic accounts of this period clearly reveal
the general growth and wealth of the country.
This increased prosperity and stability allowed a
broader spectrum of society to achieve greater
prestige and political power. Their desire for an
outward manifestation of this new-found status
was the flouting of the most expensive and
elaborate clothes and furnishings.

Against this background of enormous personal
ambition, English domestic embroidery began to
flourish. Every item of clothing, every piece of
furniture, every corner of the home was
considered for the embroiderer's embellishments

– rich with silks, spangles, gold, pearls and jewels.
The Elizabethan embroiderers, no longer content
to use Blackwork merely for decorative
trimmings, transformed it into a style which was
inherently English. The love of curvilinear plant
forms, which had been expressed in the coiling
stems of medieval illuminated manuscripts and
Celtic art, began to dominate Elizabethan
embroidery. The geometric patterns played a
complementary part as intensely rich and ornate
fillings on leaves and flowers. Designs became
ever more expansive, reflecting the exciting
tempo of the times and underlining a sense of
well-being, a love of England and a thirst for
knowledge of the New World.

The general advancement in the economic
growth of the country allowed the Elizabethans
the time and the means to pursue the exchange
of ideas and learning. Whilst her navy sailed in
search of new territories and their promised
wealth, England's scholars turned to Renaissance
Europe, eager to bring to England new ideas and
philosophies. The desire for knowledge saw the
importation of many foreign books and
pamphlets which were quickly absorbed into the
English culture. The herbal and medicinal works
of Matthioli, Dodeons, Rambert D'Alechamps
and Fuchs, and the bestiaries of Gesner and
Topsell found an eager audience.

The Elizabethans, bombarded by all these
stimuli, began to look afresh at the plants and
trees they knew so well in their own gardens, and,
despite all, it was these they favoured most as a
source for designs. The beasts and birds in
Elizabethan embroidery may occasionally seem
rare and exotic, but it is the flowers and fruits of
an English garden which play the most prominent
part. The newly acquired herbals were a constant
source of reference for the accurate portrayal of
the plants and their overwhelming influence is
seen in the surviving examples of Blackwork from
the mid 16th century.

One particular group of Blackwork
embroideries stems directly from popular
publications of the engraved prints of flowers,
fruits, birds and beasties circulating during the

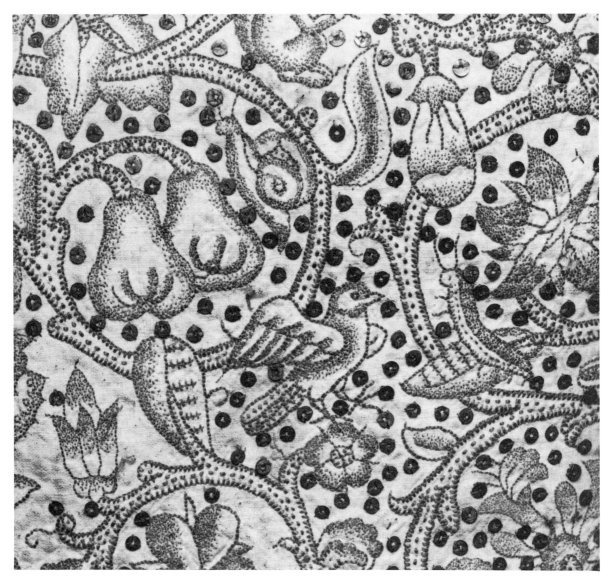

Detail of a coif from The Victoria and Albert Museum, showing the use of speckling.

16th century. Instead of the geometric patterns, the design elements of these embroideries were filled with 'speckling', tiny seeding stitches carefully graded in intensity to emulate the tones of the illustrations. Surviving pieces of Blackwork indicate that speckling was used on a variety of articles, including jackets, nightcaps, forehead cloths, hoods and coifs, until well into the first quarter of the 17th century. The detail of a coif shown in the illustration above is an exceptional example of speckling. Worked in red silk rather than the customary black, this piece from the Victoria and Albert Museum displays the consummate skill of the embroiderer in translating the effect of the printed image into embroidery.

Blackwork Pillowcover

Antony House, Cornwall

For colour illustration of project see plate 7

The pillowcover shown here, from the collection of Sir John Carew-Pole shows the superb use of both geometric fillings and free flowing elements. A. J. B. Wace says of this piece 'from its condition, its exquisite workmanship and its well composed design it ranks as one of the finest pieces of Elizabethan Blackwork in existence.'

The pillowcover, to judge from its place in the inventories of large households, was an important feature of the bed furnishings at a time when the bedroom was the most prestigious focal point of the house.

Researches have revealed that the sources of design for this pillowcover and the two

embroideries that follow can be related to particular patterns presented in the folio publications of Thomas Trevelyon (illustrated here with the relevant pieces). Although his *Miscellany* and *Commonplace* folios were not published until 1608 and 1616, the patterns are so closely connected that we can only suggest that Trevelyon's designs were available in sheet form before these dates. Alternatively, since Trevelyon had the reputation of being a copyist, he had perhaps acquired these patterns from the popular prints and broadsheets of the Elizabethan period.

Other groups of Blackwork became enriched by the use of a wider choice of stitches. Holbein stitch and backstitch were reserved for the diaper fillings whilst stem, coral, running, herringbone, trellis and buttonhole stitches were used to give expression to the new, freer designs.

Illustration from Thomas Trevelyon's *Miscellany* relating to the design on the pillowcover.

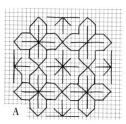
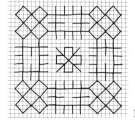
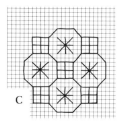
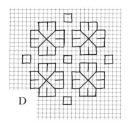

Blackwork pillow cover. Finished size 8″ × 6¼″. Stitches used: broad chain stitch, running stitch, trellis stitch, tailor's buttonhole stitch, backstitch filling patterns. 6 strands of black silk thread throughout except for the filling stitches which are worked with one strand.

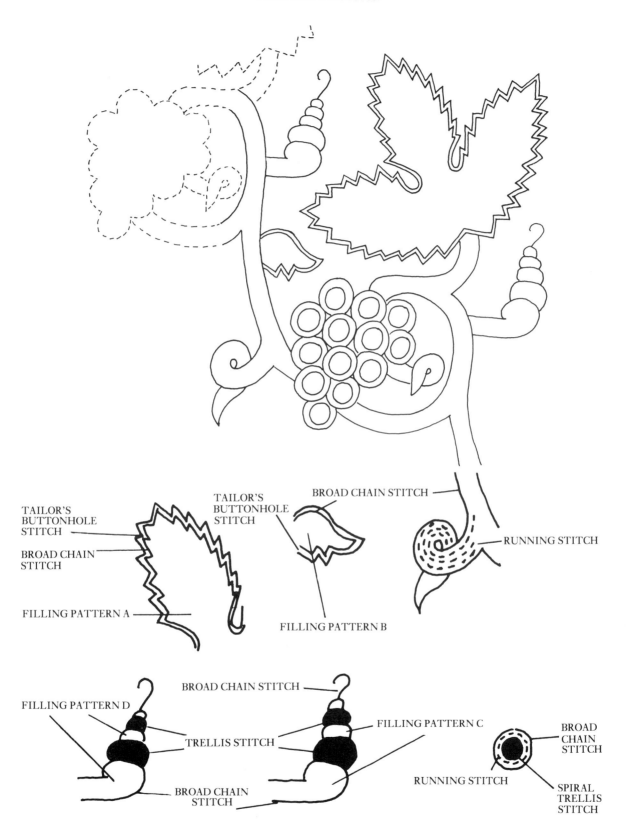

TAILOR'S
BUTTONHOLE
STITCH

TAILOR'S
BUTTONHOLE
STITCH

BROAD CHAIN STITCH

BROAD CHAIN
STITCH

RUNNING STITCH

FILLING PATTERN A

FILLING PATTERN B

FILLING PATTERN D

BROAD CHAIN STITCH

TRELLIS STITCH

FILLING PATTERN C

BROAD
CHAIN
STITCH

BROAD CHAIN
STITCH

RUNNING STITCH

SPIRAL
TRELLIS
STITCH

Blackwork Panel

Metropolitan Museum of Art, New York

For colour illustration of project see plate 8

Illustration from Thomas Trevelyon's *Miscellany* relating to the design of blackwork panel.

In many cases geometric fillings were entirely forsaken in Blackwork design. The panel from the Metropolitan Museum in New York illustrated opposite, which dates from toward the latter end of the 16th century, shows this further direction of Blackwork embroidery. The design of interlacing strapwork (itself reminiscent of earlier Blackwork), with interstices filled with flowers and grapes, was widely used on skirt fronts and sleeves throughout the Elizabethan period. This lovely piece exemplifies how, with a few well chosen stitches – buttonhole with a little fishbone stitch and stem stitch – the embroiderer could achieve a strength of design and a variety of texture.

Late 16th century blackwork panel from the Metropolitan Museum of Art.

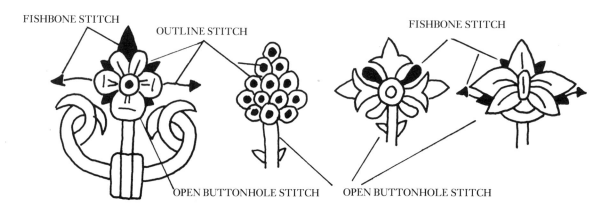

FISHBONE STITCH

OUTLINE STITCH

FISHBONE STITCH

OPEN BUTTONHOLE STITCH

OPEN BUTTONHOLE STITCH

Blackwork panel from the Metropolitan Museum of Art.
Finished size 10″ × 8¾″. Worked in open buttonhole stitch,
outline stitch and fishbone stitch on medium weight white
linen, using two strands of black silk thread.

Silk Coverlet

Victoria and Albert Museum, London

For colour illustration of project see plate 9

A counterpart to the austere yet rich Blackwork on white linen was the magnificent elaboration of gold and coloured silk embroidery favoured toward the end of the 16th century. These sumptuous embroideries, worked on dress as well as furnishings, proved to be a perfect means by which the Elizabethan could indulge his obsessive love of ostentation. English embroidery reached the heights of fantastic visual extravagance, a testimony to how far the Elizabethan would go to make himself and his home the envy of the world. The coverlet shown here illustrates the scale and extent to which these embroideries could be taken. The delicate design of English flowers contained within coiling stems of goldwork achieves a beautifully rich visual harmony.

Illustration from Thomas Trevelyon's *Miscellany* relating to the design of the coverlet.

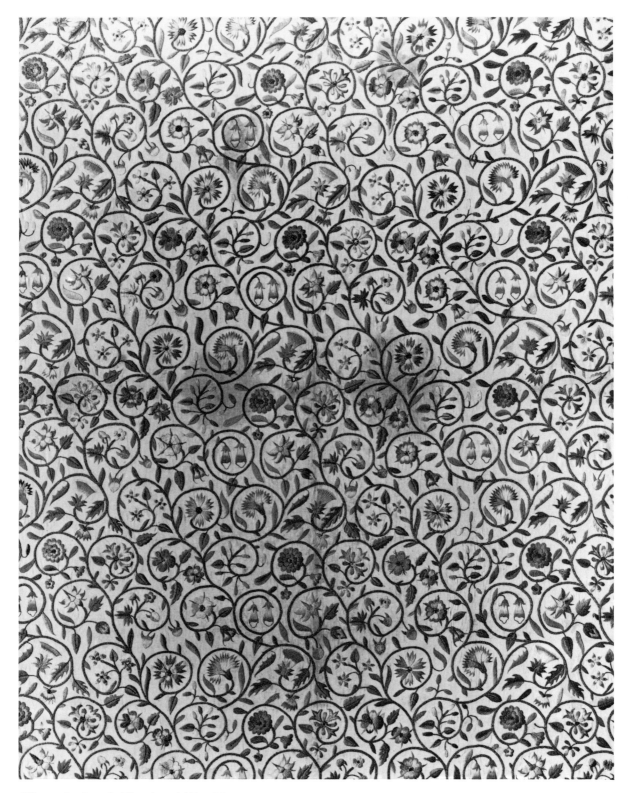

Silk coverlet from the Victoria and Albert Museum.

Coverlet

Coverlet from Victoria and Albert Museum. Embroidery worked on linen ground using DMC silks, Fil or DMC gold thread and tiny black sequins. Stitches used: long and short stitch, French knots, stem stitch, broad chain. Gold tendrils first stitched in broad chain, and then outlined in stem stitch. Finished size 12″ × 12″. Detailed patterns overleaf.

MATERIALS USED
DMC SILKS:

312	501	640	733	734	832	834
841	842	843	928	3024	3042	3045	3046
3047	3052	3053	3064

FIL OR DMC GOLD THREAD
TINY BLACK SEQUINS

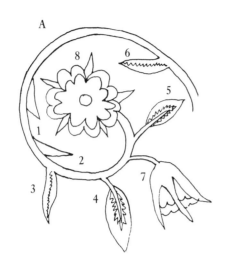

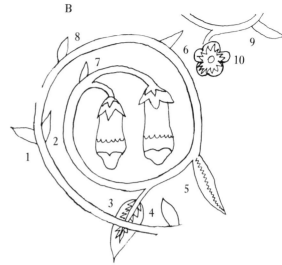

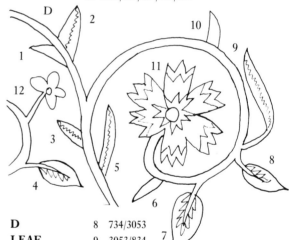

A
LEAF

1 3053
2 734
3 734 AND 3053
4 3052 AND 733
5 3052 AND 733
6 734 AND 733
7 3053/644/842/3064

ROSE BUD

ROSE

8 644/3064/BLACK SEQUINS
   OR BEADS IN CENTRE

STAMENS 3046

B
LEAF

1 3053
2 733
3 3052/834
4 3053
5 733/501
6 734

7 3053
8 3052
9 3052

FLOWER

10 3046/3045/BLACK SEQUIN IN CENTRE

FOXGLOVES

11 FROM TOP AND DOWN
12 3053/734/644/841/842

C
LEAF

1 3053/734
2 3053/734/3052
3 3053/734
4 734/3053
5 3052
6 3052

FLOWER

FROM OUTER EDGE IN
   841/312/928

BUD FROM STEM TO TIP

8 3052/734/312/928/3024

D
LEAF

1 501/733
2 733/3053
3 734/644
4 734/3052
5 734/3047
6 734
7 3053/734

8 734/3053
9 3053/834
10 3052

FLOWER

11 FROM OUTER EDGE IN 842/928/644/834
    CENTRE BLACK SEQUINS

TINY FLOWER

12 842

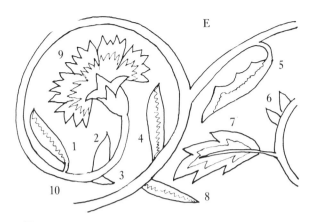

E

LEAF

1 3053/734
2 3053
3 3053
4 3053/501
5 501/733
6 501
7 501/733
8 733/5053

FLOWER

9 OUTER EDGE IN
3064/644/734/3053

F

LEAF

1 843
2 843/3053
3 843/3053
4 733/3053
5 3053/834
6 501/3052

FLOWER PETALS A B C D

7 A 640/842/928
B 841/644/928/644

C 640/842/3042/928
D 3024/928

STAMENS 3046

8 A 640/644/928
B 841/3045/3046
C 841/644/842
D 841/3045/3046

STAMENS 3046

G

LEAF AND BUDS

1 733
2 3053
3 3053
4 3064
5 644
6 3064
7 3053/734
8 3053

9 644
10 733/501
11 3064
12 644
13 640
14 644
15 3064
16 640

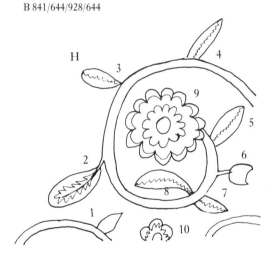

H

LEAVES

1 3052
2 3052/734
3 3053/734
4 3053
5 734/3053
6 3053
7 3053/501

8 3053/734
FLOWER FROM OUTER EDGE IN
9 3045/3046/832/3046
BLACK SEQUINS IN CENTRE
TINY FLOWER
10 3064/644

4 SAMPLERS

Samplers have been the subject of countless studies for as long as needlework itself has interested historians. The function of samplers, their stylistic and geographical differences, the images and variety of stitches employed, and their relationship to contemporary embroidery make them fascinating on many levels. The original development of samplers as a necessary reference for patterns, and their later educational applications have endowed them with a curiously personal quality, adding a further dimension to their many undoubted attractions.

Before the advent of printing brought with it a steady supply of pattern books, embroiderers noted their repertoire of patterns on a piece of cloth, and this rich treasury of ideas formed their 'aide memoire' to be referred to and added to as time went on. This sampler would also be used to try out new patterns, perhaps selected from a broderer's drawings or pattern sheets.

Throughout history samplers must have performed this function wherever a tradition of embroidery existed. Indeed, fragments of Egyptian embroidery, dating from between 200 and 500 AD, displaying motifs of birds, animals and fishes have been tentatively classified as samplers, and it could be assumed that others from this and later periods have been lost through the ages. It is, however, only from the late 16th century onwards that a sufficient number of samplers exist for there to be absolute certainty about their classification. The earliest dated English sampler, thus far known, in the collection at the Victoria and Albert Museum, was worked in 1598 by Jane Bostocke and there are very few undated samplers which could, with any accuracy, be dated earlier than this.

The earliest reference to a sampler in England occurs in the household accounts of Elizabeth of York (died 1503), Queen of Henry VII, 'an ell of lynnyn for a sampler for the Queen.' Shakespeare, always topical in his metaphors and imagery, mentions samplers in at least two of his plays, indicating that the sampler was widely recognised by the middle of the 16th century. It is our loss that there are no visual records for us to see and we can only wonder at how these samplers may have looked.

The clearest definition of how an early sampler was used is given by Barnabe Rich in *Of Phylotus and Emilia* published in 1591. This short passage creates a vivid picture of the Elizabethan embroiderer setting out to plan her work.

'Now when she had dines she might go to seek out her exemplers, and to peruse which worke doe beste in a ruffe, whiche in a gorget, whiche in a sleeve, whiche in a quaife, whiche in a cante, whiche in a handcarcheef, what lace would doe beste to edge it, whate seame, whate stitche, whate cutte, whate garde; and to sitte her doune and take it furthe by little and little and thus with her nedle to passe the after noone with devising things of her owne wearynge.'

In the 16th century, domestic embroidery was a flourishing art and the role of the amateur embroiderer was of considerable importance. Samplers of this period must have been worked in abundance by women and girls, whose accomplishments in embroidery reached new heights as clothing became ever more elaborate and rich. Those few samplers which can be judged to be from the 16th century, show a wealth of motifs; birds, flowers, insects, animals, fruits, as well as decorative borders. Worked in brightly coloured silks and with lavish use of gold and silver thread, they reflect the style and sumptuous extravagance of the contemporary dress and furnishings.

The printed pattern book, which was to have such an impact on embroidery, made its first appearance in the early 16th century. Johannes Schönsperger, son of a printing family of Augsburg, Germany, himself a paper mill owner and textile printer, combined his talents and facilities to publish in 1523, *Furm oder Modelbuchlein*. This first of all pattern books contained Schönsperger's woodblock prints of patterns for both weaving and a variety of embroidery techniques. This was quickly followed in 1524 by *Ein New Modelbuch* also published by Schönsperger, and containing further patterns. These two books were so well received that other printers began to publish the patterns themselves under their own titles. In 1527 Peter Quentel alone published four separate editions, all copies of the Schönsperger originals. Antonio Tagliente, of Venice added oriental motifs and thus initiated the publishing of pattern books in Italy.

The earliest English pattern book was published in London by Adrian Poyntz in 1591, but contained nothing new. *New and Singular patternes and works of linnen* was an English version of Federigo Vinciola's book of the same name. Further plagiarisms were published in England but the first book to have an unmistakeably English character was Richard Shoreleyker's *A Schole House for the Needle*, published in 1624. Alongside copies from Quentel, Ostaus, Sibmacher and Flötner were Shoreleyker's own drawings of 'Sundry sortes of spots, as flowers, birdes and fishes etc' with wild strawberry, rose, pansy, thistle and pea pod so typical of Elizabethan and Jacobean embroidery. The single sheets of wood cuts produced by Peter Stent and John Overton, though enjoying enormous popularity in the 17th century, could not compete with the wide circulation of the printed book. John Boler's *The Needles Excellency*

of 1634 became what one can only call in today's terms a best seller, running to no fewer than twelve editions.

During the first half of the 17th century, the wider availability of pattern books began to change the original concept of the sampler. Its role as a record was less important and it gradually became a testament to the embroiderer's considerable expertise. Typical 17th century samplers display row after row of open and cut work designs, in imitation of the lace which was such a feature of their dress, together with bands of Italianate borders of stylised flowers, fruit and foliage, and whitework. Spot motifs are also a common feature, whether they are of diaper and interlaced strapwork designs or detached sprays of flowers, animals, birds and insects. The influence of the pattern books is clearly seen in the repetition of certain designs and motifs on various samplers. Throughout the century the quality of the embroidery became more and more intricate as the embroiderers sought after perfection and acclaim.

Young girls were obliged to learn the art of embroidery from an early age and it is no wonder that they were proud to add both their names and ages to their samplers. The excellence of their work bears witness to how highly embroidery was valued as a most desirable accomplishment. Treasured samplers were handed down to younger generations who were encouraged to learn the skills of their mothers. Thus the sampler became a lesson in technique – a tradition which lasted through the 19th century, when no girl's education was considered complete until she had worked her sampler to everyone's satisfaction. Patterns no longer reflected contemporary taste, but rather prolonged the life of otherwise unused designs. The repertoire of stitches used to create the sampler diminished and the wide variety of stitches seen on the samplers of the 17th century gave way to the almost exclusive use of cross stitch.

Since embroidery was an important part of the curriculum of all girls' educational establishments in the 19th century, a certain uniformity of style and presentation crept into the samplers produced. The most typical 19th century English samplers show verses or moral texts, often of a rather gloomy nature, surrounded by unrelated birds, flowerpots, stylised trees and flowers, with the occasional house, all neatly arranged within an undulating border of floral ornament. Whilst wealthy pupils would work upon perfecting their ability to produce the finest of work, less fortunate girls would work row after row of neat alphabets, preparing them for future service in the marking of household linens.

Dutch Sampler

Openluchtmuseum, Arnhem, Netherlands

For colour illustration of project see plate 15

Comprehensive collections of samplers, such as those at the Victoria and Albert Museum and the Cooper-Hewitt Museum, contain wonderfully preserved examples from many origins. Italy, Spain, Germany, the Netherlands, Scandinavia and America amongst others, produced generation after generation of samplers of remarkable beauty, and endless fascinating comparisons can be made between their presentation and imagery. Samplers from the Netherlands are extraordinarily diverse, displaying very distinctive regional characteristics. Large, decorative alphabets beautifully outlined with filigree curlicues make the samplers of Friesland immediately recognisable. The letters are often dispersed randomly across the work and interspaced with equally decorative diamond motifs of every size.

Other Dutch samplers rely on religious themes such as the Passion, Adam and Eve and the Tree of Knowledge, The Spies of Canaan and the Five Wise and the Five Foolish Virgins. Often political motifs were used as the main focal point. 'The Maid in the Garden' and the 'Garden of Holland' relate to the House of Orange, whilst the 'Dutch Lion' symbolises the Union of the Seven Provinces of the Netherlands.

The Island of Marken in North Holland has a long tradition of the most beautiful needlework which was, and still is, applied to household linens and to their wonderfully ornate costumes. The samplers of Marken are exquisite and have a distinct format of both large and small motifs worked all over the main body of the sampler with a broad band of densely worked border patterns running down one side. The sampler shown opposite from the Netherlands Openluchtmuseum in Arnhem, worked by Annetje Muiesdochter in 1663, is typical. Until the reclamation of the Zuyder Zee, the Island of Marken was quite isolated from the rest of Holland and the patterns for many forms of needlework practised there would have been handed round a relatively small group of people. This would account for the frequent repetition of certain motifs and for the existence of at least two other samplers of the 17th century which are so remarkably similar to this of Annetje

Muiesdochter. One wonders if she had as her model the sampler of 1640, which displays more than twelve identical motifs. The large square motif with roses at each side appears on the oldest existing sampler known in Holland, whilst curiously, the Fleur de Lys motif has been identified on an Icelandic Altar Frontal in the National Museum of Iceland, dated 1617. The border patterns were of considerable importance as they formed an integral part of the traditional costume of Marken up to the present day. Each pattern has its significance whether used on the neckband of a bride's dress, on apron strings or the long ribbons of the cap where special ribbons are reserved for certain festivals and holidays.

⚡	355 D
L L	833 D
⫽	733 D
W	3045 D
• •	0922 A
▲ ▲	0844 A
↑ ↑	839 D
⁄⁄	842 D

A = Anchor
D = DMC

Dutch sampler. Finished size 14″ × 8¾″.
Worked in cross stitch and long armed cross
stitch on evenweave linen 34 threads to the
inch, using two threads of Anchor and DMC
stranded embroidery cotton.

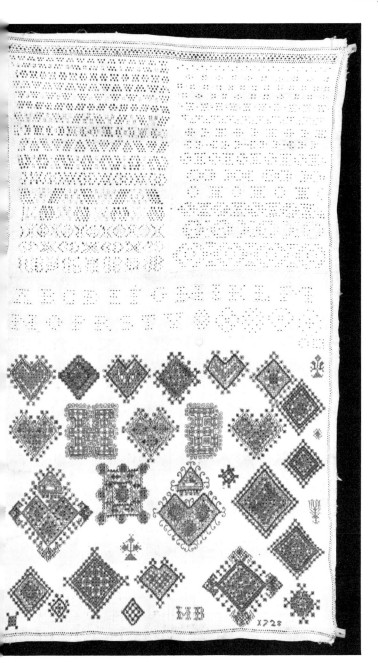

The designs used on these borders are made up of zig-zag lines and triangles, and have an interesting relationship to the O X O patterns so often found in the knitting of the Fair Isles. The dispersal of these lovely patterns throughout the seafaring nations underlines the international language of design. Indeed these same patterns are used repeatedly on an English sampler in the extensive collection at the Fitzwilliam Museum in Cambridge (left). Here they are worked in whitework and bands of them are displayed above the spot motifs of diamonds reminiscent of those found on samplers of Friesland.

Early 18th century English sampler from The Fitzwilliam Museum in Cambridge.

Vierlande Sampler

Cooper-Hewitt Museum, New York

For colour illustration of project see plate 11

Two motifs found again and again in samplers from all over Europe are the garland and the Tree of Life. Samplers showing an almost exclusive use of these were worked in Vierlande, a region of North Germany. Traditionally embroidered throughout in black silk and cross stitch, circular garlands of all sizes with the delicate intricacy of snowflakes are placed all over the linen ground interspersed with delightful Tree of Life motifs and diamonds. The overall effect is far from sombre and these samplers have a joyous, harmonious quality. The Tree of Life has been a recurring element of embroidery and textile design from the earliest times. The Egyptians, Greeks and Turks have portrayed it in one form or another and it appears in the designs of India, Persia, the Middle East and all over Northern Europe. Though it has been an important part of the many diverse cultures, the symbolism attached to the motif has remained remarkably constant. The Tree of Life is a symbol of eternity, of renewal and the breath of life itself. No importance was attached to what kind of tree it should be and perhaps this is why it could be so easily adapted to many different forms of design.

The Vierlande sampler opposite shows the Tree of Life in a very stylised form. Flanked from top to bottom by birds it is very typical of the way in which the motif was treated throughout Europe and in particular in Holland where it often appeared on the betrothal kerchiefs which were an important part of the courtship ritual (photograph below).

A 17th century Dutch betrothal kerchief showing a beautiful example of the tree of life motif.

Sampler from Vierlande. Finished size approximately 8″ × 7″. Worked in cross stitch on linen evenweave, 30 threads to the inch, using black silk.

Herbal Panel

Hardwick Hall, Derbyshire

For colour illustration of project see plate 12

The 16th century could be considered as the first age when domestic architecture began to develop in England. It was a period which saw the rapid rise of an ever-increasing number of gentry to the top echelons of society, both in rank and wealth, either through their own endeavours or through royal favour. With their new-found status they needed to consolidate their position in society with a home that both proclaimed and reflected their rank. It became necessary not only to impress their immediate neighbours, but also to be host to others of equal rank in a manner fitting to their class. Their homes became splendid monuments to their self-claimed superiority and were built to be remarkable and to astonish guests.

Interiors were considered of equal importance to exteriors and were lavishly decorated. Architects and designers, armed with the influences and ideas of the Renaissance in Europe, were eager to build and found ready clients in the newly rich.

Hardwick Hall was built in the late 16th century to satisfy the ambition of one remarkable woman – the Countess of Shrewsbury, or Bess of Hardwick. True to this age of tremendous endeavour and exuberance, Bess of Hardwick showed throughout her long life an overwhelming ability to grasp whatever came her way and to use it for the betterment of herself and her family. From a relatively inauspicious background, she contrived through four advantageous marriages to acquire enormous wealth and power. This extraordinary woman left the most magnificent legacy in buildings, furnishings and embroideries.

During her marriage to her fourth husband, George Talbot, 6th Earl of Shrewsbury, Bess had the running of six houses, including Chatsworth which she acquired from her second husband, Sir William Cavendish. Her boundless obsession with rebuilding and refurbishing was given ample scope and she was more than able to meet the challenge. It was late in her life, after separation from Talbot, that she was able to buy back from her brother her old family home of Hardwick. Bess immediately embarked on a scheme of rebuilding. After the death of Talbot, and even while the first mansion was incomplete, at the age of seventy, she set about the building of Hardwick Hall. The sheer scale and range of her interests and her prodigious energy can still be felt at Hardwick, but above all it is her overriding passion for embroidery which shines out.

75

16th century panel from Hardwick Hall featuring the date palm.

3371	D		611	D		937	D
733	D		0887	A		0393	A
0945	A		833	D		0831	A
0879	A		834	D		3023	D
471	D		0886	A		613	D
0878	A		0265	A		3363	D
470	D		822	D			
3012	D		0843	A			
831	D		0922	A			
371	D		0379	A			

ALL UNMARKED AND BACKGROUND = 822

D = DMC   A = ANCHOR

Hardwick Hall panel. Finished size $12\frac{1}{2}'' \times 13\frac{1}{2}''$. Worked in cross stitch on double canvas, 15 threads to the inch, using 6 strands of Anchor and DMC stranded embroidery cotton.

A date palm engraving from Matthioli's herbal.

household at this time) who would have been called upon to assist with drawing out patterns and overseeing the larger projects. However, the most interesting items of embroidery are those which bear her own personal monogram – a large ES, conspicuously placed. Among the embroideries so proudly marked, the panels featured here, depicting plants and trees, are of great importance and their intrinsic beauty reveals itself at once.

Each plant is beautifully balanced within an octagonal border containing a Latin motto. From the translation of these it would seem that Bess was more concerned with how they looked, than with what they meant. They bear little relationship to the plants and were perhaps put in to impress the onlooker with a liberal sprinkling of Latin. However, the fine drawing underlying the embroideries gives this group a remarkable strength and clarity. The relative simplicity and refinement of the pieces makes them stand out in contrast with the more elaborate embroideries around them.

The designs for the octagons are clearly based on the engravings in the herbal of Pietro Andrea Matthioli, published in Venice in 1568, and Lyon in 1572. Many of the plants, including the date palm above can be traced to this source. The embroideries parallel the illustrations so closely that it must be concluded that either a copy of this book was available to Bess or that someone close to her had intimate knowledge of the publication.

Bess herself was an accomplished needlewoman and, without doubt, there are many pieces in the embroidery collection at Hardwick that can be directly attributed to her. Records show that Bess had in her employ a professional embroiderer (a common custom in any great

Oxburgh Hangings

Oxburgh Hall, Norfolk

For colour illustration of project see plate 13

At the time that the Hardwick panels were being carried out, Mary Queen of Scots was in the charge of the Earl of Shrewsbury (she was under his guardianship for fifteen years, from 1569 to 1584). Despite the strain and expense of being responsible for Mary, Shrewsbury was happy to report 'This Queen contriveth daily to resort unto my wife's chamber where with Lady Lewiston and Mrs Seton useth to sit working with the needle . . .' The enforced association of Bess and Mary was initially eased by their mutual love of embroidery. Mary's superior education and her French upbringing brought new horizons to Bess and her embroideries began to reflect the taste of the Scottish Queen for working small panels. It would be reasonable to suppose that at this point Bess and Mary were planning and working together on the small embroideries which make up the Oxburgh hangings. These hangings consist of three large panels of green velvet to which numerous embroideries worked by Bess and Mary have been applied.

This joint venture in embroidery, thought to have been carried out between 1569 and 1584, provides the most superb visual testimony to the friendship which initially existed between these two ladies, despite the fact that they were constrained together under such extraordinary circumstances.

Collectively the three panels are so closely related both in style and content that they must be viewed as having been intended for a single purpose. Each panel nonetheless holds a character of its own, and they are known as the Marion hanging, the Shrewsbury hanging and the Cavendish hanging. These hangings display various small cross stitch embroideries, cruciform or octagon shaped, arranged around a dominant central embroidered square of emblematic design. It is the personal elements contained within these emblematic embroideries which so subtly define not only the character of each hanging but also the difference between that of Bess and that of Mary. For instance, in the central square of the Marion hanging, Mary has cleverly embroidered in tent stitch an arrangement of symbols and emblems and a motto 'virtue flourishes by a wound', which alludes to her captivity, whilst on the Cavendish and Shrewsbury hangings Bess selected emblematic motifs and mottoes which refer to her grief on the death of her second husband (Cavendish) and to the power and ingenuity of herself and her husband at the time (Shrewsbury). Only fragments now exist of a fourth panel, and these remaining pieces can be seen at the Victoria and Albert Museum. It is known that these panels were adapted, about a hundred years after they were first made, to form bedhangings, and it would have been then that the fourth panel was cut up to provide a valance for the bed.

The Oxburgh hangings not only account for the major surviving portion of embroideries which can be unquestionably attributed to Mary Queen of Scots (some thirty small panels bear

Mary's initials or monogram) but also indicate the staggering proportions of the output of embroidery that Bess and Mary achieved together.

The hangings were an extraordinary undertaking for the two women stitched well over a hundred separate pieces, each one in itself a curious little silk embroidery in fresh natural colours. Many of the designs they chose tend towards the eccentric – strange birds and fishes, entwined snakes, a crocodile, relieved only by a few flowers and trees. Juxtaposed as they are on the green velvet of the hangings they create a wonderfully cluttered and jewel-like impact and present the most impressive and definitive record of their virtuosity in the art of needlework. The source material for most of the creatures and plants is recognised as Gesner's *Icones Animalium* and again Matthioli's herbal. There are certain motifs on the Oxburgh hangings which appear several times elsewhere, and there must have been a healthy interchange of ideas between embroiderers, professional and otherwise. It is likely that Bess adopted the image of the date palm after Mary's established use of it, not only on the Marion hanging but also, more importantly, as the reverse of the Mary Rial, a Scottish coin struck in 1566 (below).

The Mary Rial coin, which shows an earlier use of a similar date palm.

The Marion hanging, Oxburgh Hall.

Detail of a tiger from the Marion hanging.

COLOUR KEY

	DMC/ANCHOR BLACK			ANCHOR (
	ANCHOR 0905			DMC 832
	ANCHOR 0162			DMC 733
	ANCHOR 0851			DMC 928
	DMC 924			DMC 927
	DMC 610			ANCHOR (
	DMC 611			DMC 644
	ANCHOR 0393			DMC 613
	ANCHOR 0898			

The Oxburgh hanging. Worked on 14 hole double canvas in cross stitch, using Anchor and DMC embroidery silks. Finished size approximately $8\frac{1}{2}'' \times 8\frac{1}{2}''$. Finished embroidery to be applied to a ground fabric.

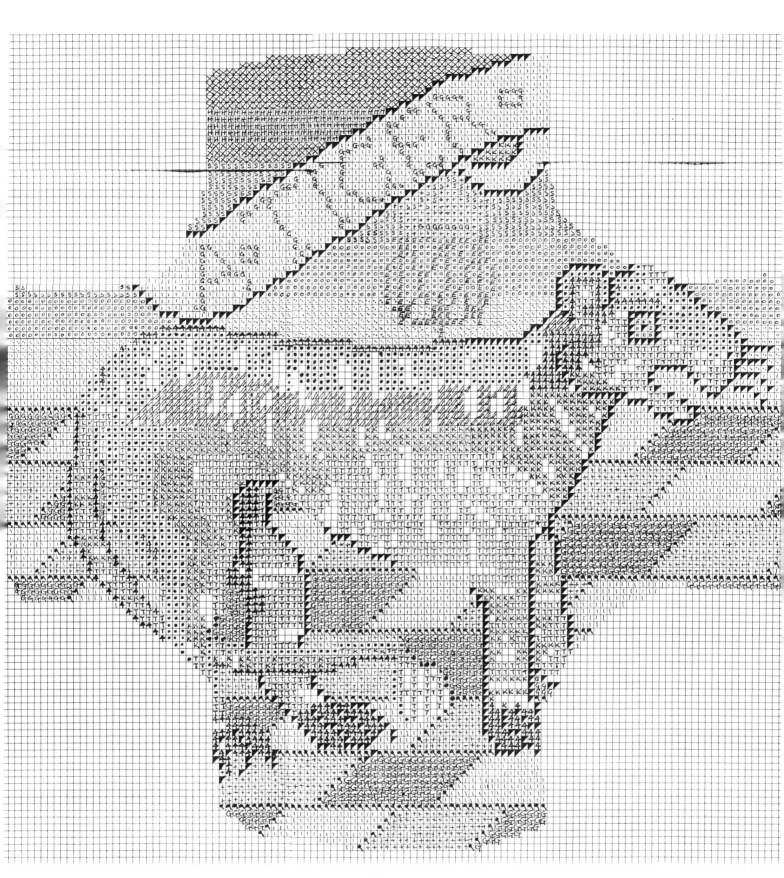

83

Embroidered panel from Traquair House. Many of the animals featured on it are directly comparable with those on the Oxburgh hangings.

Further to this there are many images on the Oxburgh hangings which are also on embroidered panels at Traquair House, Scotland, the leopard being a notable example (above).

There is no documentary evidence that Mary was directly involved in working the panels of embroidered flowers, birds and animals at Traquair House. However, there is a close similarity between these and the Oxburgh hangings. No fewer than ten birds and animals can be identified as common to both, and indeed the same source material of Gesner's *Icones Animalium* must have been used. Although the Traquair panels have been dated at about 1610, the design of the panels suggests that they are contemporary with Mary's work. The Queen's inventory at Chartley in 1586 includes, amongst countless other pieces, at least 360 embroideries of a similar type.

The Traquair embroideries are truly remarkable. They are in a wonderful state of preservation, still uncut but ready to be applied to silk or velvet. They allow a rare opportunity to glimpse the original glowing colours of Elizabethan embroidery and present a multitude of images which vividly bring to mind the glorious ground of a millefleur tapestry.

Once again the herbals play their part. The engravings of Matthioli can be clearly identified in the fruits and flowers. By the end of the 16th century it was quite common for the professional broderer to refer to herbals and bestiaries to gather material for embroidery designs. Amateur embroiderers would use them too if they were fortunate enough to possess copies.

Emblems, anagrams and fables were also favourite devices used by Mary in much of her work. She is known to have had French

Leopard illustration from Topsell woodblocks.

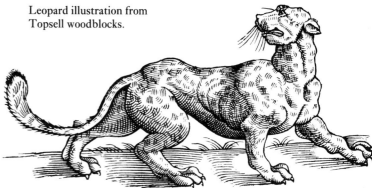

Above: detail of coverlet at Hardwick Hall.
Right: Topsell's woodblock of the stork and snake.

embroiderers as part of her entourage. Pierre Oudry and Charles Plouvart must surely have kept her acquainted with the current fashions in France, for an image on another of her embroideries repeats that on a French valance (above left). Coincidentally, the same bird and snake appear in an oval on the coverlet currently at Hardwick, also illustrated here.

Mary's involvement with embroidery is so renowned that it would be easy to assume all kinds of pieces to be hers. Inventories before and after her execution show the considerable volume of work she achieved, but only the Oxburgh Hangings and two cushion covers at Hardwick can be attributed to her with absolute certainty. The designs of the cushions feature the Thistle of Scotland, the Lily of France and the Rose of England. Imposed on these are oval medallions in which are stitched scenes depicting stories from the fables of Gabriel Faerno (first published in Rome in 1563). The images of the two frogs at the well, a cat and a cock, and a bird attacking a snake are very close indeed to the engravings in Faerno's book.

85

Long Panel

For colour illustration of project see plate 17

Detail of an embroidered panel from The Cooper-Hewitt Museum. The complete piece features twelve fables.

The *Emblem* book of Geoffrey Whitney was much admired by the Elizabethans. A folio edition was presented to Robert, Earl of Leicester, at the time of his departure to the Low Countries. The reception of this edition, by all who saw it, was such that Whitney was begged to have it printed and thus the first edition was published at Leyden in 1553. The book features delightful engravings, each illustrating a tale told beneath it in verse. The emblems deal with honour, pride, envy, corruption, drunkenness, courtesy, virtue and piety, and their morality can always be applied in several ways. Thus the fox rejecting the grapes which are too high for him to reach alludes to those who, unable to attain the heights to which they aspire, make mockery of them. Likewise the stork feeding its young illustrates an elegant verse advocating filial and parental love. The stork with a snake in his beak appears in many early Christian illustrations, emphasising a further aspect of its symbolism. As an eater of snakes, the stork was seen as the devourer of evil and defender of Christianity, symbolising piety and vigilance. The *Emblemata* of Florentius Schoonhovius features the stork in this context. The image of the stork and snake is found in a number of embroideries of the 16th century. The coverlet featuring the Banquet of Lucretia (below) has borders composed of strapwork enclosing rectangular compartments. These contain animals and birds amidst trees laden with fruit. A rectangle in the upper border depicts the stork and snake beneath roses and fruit trees in an almost identical manner to that found on an embroidery in the Cooper-Hewitt Museum in New York (opposite page). Made from two valances sewn together, this panel is designed to display twelve fables or emblems. Each one, worked in cross stitch in wool with highlights of silk, is exquisitely drawn with animals set against a background of fruiting trees encased within borders of coiling stems and flowers. The valances are thought to be French, circa 1600, and certainly the superb quality of the design and workmanship reflects the very best of French professionalism and taste.

Detail of a tablecarpet of The Banquet of Lucretia, showing another snake and crane.

⁄⁄	971	ZZ	911	VV	972 ANCHOR			
‡‡	985	∩∩	122	⁄⁄	0956 ANCHOR			
⁄⁄	975	33	183	LL	0945 ANCHOR			
↑↑	125	‖‖	981	77	734 DMC			
VV	294	⊘⊘	929	::	842 DMC			
55	973	WW	325	ıı	422 DMC			
XX	548	⁄⁄	158	::	613 DMC			
KK	326	::	346	◣◢	BLACK			
⊘⊘	921	▲▲	644					
⊗⊗	302	++	952					

Detail from embroidered panel in the Cooper-Hewitt Museum. Finished size $10\frac{5}{8}'' \times 9\frac{5}{8}''$. Worked in cross stitch on double canvas, 12 threads to the inch, using 6 strands of Anchor and DMC stranded embroidery cotton and two strands of Appleton's crewel wool.

88

Detail of a valance in the Metropolitan Museum of Art, which demonstrates the genre style in embroidery.

The importance of the valance in the scheme of decorative furnishings cannot be overstressed. It was the one part of the bed which afforded a flat permanent surface highly suitable for the embroiderer's art. In the 16th century valances were almost always worked in tent stitch in wool and silk. Relatively few examples survive intact considering the quantity which must have been worked, and those which can still be seen are almost always linked to a French provenance or have strong connections with Scotland.

The designs tend to fall within clear groups. Those based on Flemish engravings show scenes from Ovid's *Metamorphoses* or the Bible, with the characters assuming the highly stylised costumes of the French court. Others call upon the fables for their subject matter and a third group consists of applied sprigs and flowers. Finally there are the valances depicting everyday occupations of ordinary folk. These designs are known as 'genre'.

6 GENRE

Elizabeth I reigned for forty five years, until 1603, just three years into the 17th century. It is no surprise therefore to find, after such a long reign, the influence of the Elizabethan age overlapping into that of her successor, James I, thus making the boundaries between much Elizabethan and Jacobean embroidery virtually indistinguishable. The greatest legacy left to England by Elizabeth was a tremendous exuberance and sense of personal identity which would prove to be the strength needed to carry the English through the turmoil and conflict of the Civil War, half a century later. She left England a stable and prosperous nation and her positive encouragement of audacity, imagination and vitality continued to inspire writers, artists and scientists long after her death. Elizabeth actively promoted the English court into developing to the full the highly cultural atmosphere generated by her father, Henry VIII. Some of the very first theatrical productions were staged in her honour and literature soared to new heights. The arts of painting, music and embroidery likewise continued to flourish with the adventurous spirit she invoked.

It is easy to forget that the influence of the Elizabethan era, which flowered in the latter years of her reign, continued to be felt everywhere until at least twenty years after James had come to the throne. Whilst flowers and animals still dominated late Elizabethan and Jacobean embroideries, especially for dress, certain large scale canvas pieces were treated differently. The furnishings for the home (bed valances, table carpets, long cushions etc.) demanded a subject matter with more scope and a bolder approach.

The stories from the Bible, fables and mythology were a natural and familiar source to which to turn and embroideries for large household articles mirrored these long-loved themes. At the same time designers welcomed the opportunity to look anew at such favourite subjects as the hunt, the cycle of nature and the months of the year. But the most exciting innovation was seen in the development of the genre style. The term 'genre' can best be defined as a style depicting ordinary people doing ordinary things within a familiar setting. The paintings of Breughel are instantly recognized as the foremost genre paintings of the 16th century. Breughel used the genre style as a device which enabled him to comment freely on the decadent society around him. The Elizabethans certainly appreciated this aspect but preferred to use the genre format to proclaim their position in society and they took delight in embroidery designs displaying the lord and lady parading in front of their beautiful home whilst the rest of mankind was seen going about his daily work.

Contemporary engravings were an undoubted influence on both genre embroideries and tapestries and the work of Flemish painters and engravers such as Martin de Voss, Peter de Costar, Crispin Van der Passe and Breughel made a particular impression. The theme of hunting and the seasons had been an inspiration to writers and artists for centuries. Medieval manuscripts, the magnificently illustrated *Books of Hours* and psalters abound in vignettes of the labourer about his seasonal work.

A superb set of Sheldon tapestries, now at Hatfield House, depicts idealised images of

Spring, Summer, Autumn and Winter, each set against a landscape teeming with country life. *The Seasons*, a set of engravings by Martin de Voss (1531–1603), bears such a striking similarity to this tapestry suite that one can only assume that Sheldon owned copies of the prints. At Packwood House, a property once owned by the Sheldon family, there is still to be seen a roundel of stained glass bearing the De Voss image of Winter. Sheldon must have held this artist's work in great esteem and have been happy to have his work as a source for his designs.

The Royal Hunt or The Chase had been an equally well-loved and important subject, featuring in many medieval paintings and tapestries, and playing a prominent part in the mysticism of the medieval period. The Chase had symbolised the flight of the seven deadly sins – the hunter looked forward to enjoying this kingly sport in Paradise.

On a more temporal level, the hunt continued to be of great significance in providing meat in plenty after the exciting challenge of the chase. It was still a passionate preoccupation amongst the nobility of 15th and 16th century Europe as the civilised world moved toward the Renaissance. Hunts, with their elaborate ritual and grandiose style, had tremendous value as indicators of position and superiority, and they were frequently the subject of tapestries woven to adorn the walls of the nobility. The Devonshire Hunting Tapestries, formerly hung at Hardwick Hall and now in the Victoria and Albert Museum, are magnificent in their conception. Originating from workshops in Arras or Tournai between 1435 and 1450, the four tapestries feature lavishly attired nobles pursuing their quarry of deer, otter, birds and boar. They give us, still, a splendid account of this most revered of sports and are rich with the textures of rural as well as aristocratic life in the 15th century.

Embroiderers of the 16th century, rekindling their interest in the theme of the hunt, brought it to much more manageable proportions, reflecting the more homely place it occupied in English country life.

Bradford Tablecarpet

Victoria and Albert Museum, London

For colour illustration of project see plate 14 and jacket

This tablecarpet, formerly in the collection of the Earl of Bradford and now at the Victoria and Albert Museum, brings together the hunt and everyday life in what is probably the finest example of the 16th century genre style. The design is cleverly conceived with a central field of trellis covered in fruiting vine, placed so as to fall on the surface of the table. The borders containing the delightful genre scenes hang down the sides to be seen to their best advantage. These borders are filled with figures intent upon their daily work or indulging in pastoral relaxation. Set against the English countryside, with an abundance of trees, flowers, streams and country houses, they endow the carpet with a quality which is both gentle and lyrical. The workmanship is extremely fine and the carpet was probably the product of a professional workshop.

Details about the source of the designs for the borders of the Bradford Tablecarpet would be of immense interest, for they are remarkably close in character and style to certain images found in

tapestries from the Sheldon looms, which are exactly contemporary. The huntsman with his horn, the dogs chasing after, ranged in front of moated houses set against a continuous landscape, are seen in both the tablecarpet and several sets of Sheldon tapestries. Few references exist to the history of the designs used by the Sheldon weavers and one can only surmise their origins. One or two tenuous connections can be noted, however. Although the scenes in both the carpet and the tapestries appear to be very English in character, it is possible that they were influenced by contemporary European designs. Richard Hykes, who under the will of William Sheldon had control of the Sheldon workshops, had learnt his craft in the Low Countries and may have brought back these images. Certainly other designs often used in Sheldon Tapestries – the treatment of flowers, fruit and foliage in wide borders – owe their origins to Flemish tapestries of the same period.

A further link is worth exploring. William or perhaps Ralph Sheldon had had business dealings with the Countess of Shrewsbury at Hardwick Hall. In her accounts of 1592 it is stated that she 'paid Mr Sheldon's man for seventeen armes to set upon hangings. . . . and also ten shillings to hang tapestries'. Perhaps images from the hunting tapestries at Hardwick had made their impression and were carried back to be adapted by design workshops responsible for both tapestries and embroideries. Whatever their provenance, these little scenes in the tablecarpet and the Sheldon tapestries are an enchanting addition to the wide range of Elizabethan imagery.

(Above) The Bradfort Tablecarpet (detail) from The Victoria and Albert Museum.

(Below) A Sheldon tapestry valance from The Victoria and Albert Museum.

Detail from the Bradford Tablecarpet. Worked with 2
strands of Appletons crewel wool using tent stitch on 16 hole
canvas. The infilling on the blank grapes is exactly the same
as that shown. Approximate size $16'' \times 7\frac{1}{2}''$.

COLOUR KEY

582 BROWN GROUNDINGS		903 GOLDEN BROWN	
956 DRAB FAWN		902 GOLDEN BROWN	
954 DRAB FAWN		901 GOLDEN BROWN	
975 ELEPHANT		955 DRAB FAWN	
952 DRAB FAWN		244 OLIVE	
326 DULL MARINE		355 GREY GREEN	
323 DULL MARINE		333 DRAB GREEN	
923 DULL CHINA		332 DRAB GREEN	
321 DULL MARINE		985 PUTTY	
971A ELEPHANT		761 BISCUIT	
962 IRON			

Tablecarpet

Early 17th century tablecarpet depicting the story of Gombaut and Macée in the borders.

Examples of the genre style are also found on embroideries of Flemish and French origin, but the French had their own idiosyncratic view of the rural. The pastoral poetry of the Middle Ages echoed the idealised view of country life held by the wealthy people of the towns. Those who enjoyed the relative ease and comfort of living with services and amenities readily available extolled the virtues of the simple life. With little or no knowledge of the reality, they created for themselves a fantasy world in which there was no hardship, no fatigue, where nature's bounties were there for the taking and where it was always balmy summer. For these worldly people the epitome of the idealised life was the shepherd, forever languishing in the lush landscape whilst his happy sheep nibbled nearby. An 'almanac and compendium of useful information' published in 1491 was named after the shepherd as the *Kalendrier des Bergiers* and such was its popularity amongst the upper classes that it ran to several editions. This totally unreal vision of the life of the hardworking and often poverty stricken peasant reached its zenith and paradoxically its demise in the extraordinary behaviour of Marie Antoinette when, dressed as a shepherdess, she would go to the Petit Trianon to 'tend her sheep'.

A French tablecarpet in the collection at the Metropolitan Museum, New York, narrates the story of a shepherd, Gombaut, and his beloved, Macée – a shepherdess. The theme is typical of the best of the pastoral verses. Gombaut pursues his love, amidst certain ribaldry, fellow peasants play games and frolic in the bountiful countryside whilst gentlefolk look on. The story runs round the borders of the carpet, each scene enacted in little vignettes cleverly placed between trees which separate each part of the narrative in a natural way.

The central field of the carpet is composed of classical vases and cornucopias brimming with flowers and fruits of all kinds. The embroidery is finely worked in tent stitch in wool and silk and, measuring nearly five feet by nine feet, is on a

very grand scale. Though the subject matter may deal with peasants and the abundance of nature, the overall effect is one of immense sophistication.

The origins of the story of Gombaut and Macée are obscure but the verses upon which it is based were already well known in France by the 16th century. A number of tapestry workshops, notably those of Paris, had adopted the tale. A set of seven tapestries in the collection of the Duke of Buccleugh and woven in Paris between 1655 and 1662 show the 'Amours de Gombaut et

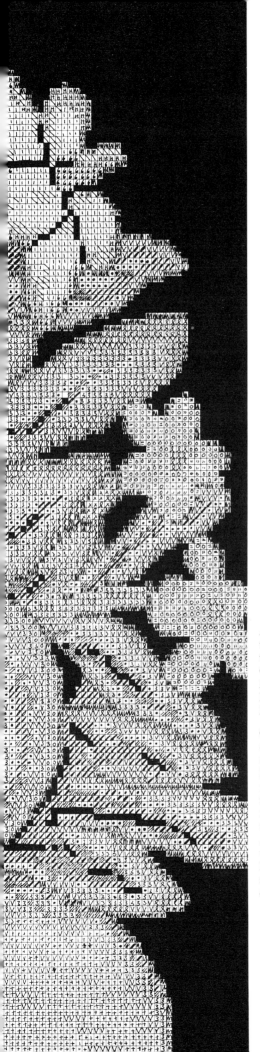

COLOUR KEY

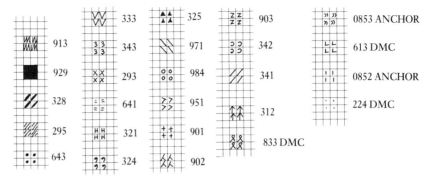

		333		325		903		0853 ANCHOR
	913		343		971		342	613 DMC
	929		293		984		341	0852 ANCHOR
	328		641		951		312	224 DMC
	295		321		901			
	643		324		902		833 DMC	

Above. The game of tiquet from the tapestry suite 'The Caves of Gombaut and Macée' Franco Flemisch Metropolitan Museum of Art.

Opposite. Tablecarpet depicting the story of Gombaut and Macée. Finished size $10\frac{1}{8}'' \times 10\frac{1}{8}''$. Worked in tent stitch on canvas, 18 threads to the inch, using 2 strands of Appleton's crewel wool, and 6 strands DMC and Anchor stranded embroidery cotton.

Macée' with panels relating the story in verse on each piece. It is thought that these or a similar set were the basis of the woodblocks published in Paris by Jean le Clerc in 1585. However, earlier versions of the tapestries are known to have existed, as an inventory made in 1531 mentions a Gombaut and Macée tapestry amongst the possessions of Floramond Robertet. Molière's somewhat derogatory mention of such tapestries brought them to the attention of linguistic scholars who believe the language of the verses to be of the 15th century at the latest. The popularity of the story reached its height between 1580 and 1620, the period of the Metropolitan embroidery.

7 CREWEL

A phenomenon of the 17th century in English needlework was the reintroduction of crewel wool embroidery. Although wool had frequently been used in embroideries throughout previous periods, generally it was worked on canvas in cross stitch or tent stitch, filling the ground completely. Surface wool embroidery of the type used on the Bayeux Tapestry had for the most part been dormant for nearly 600 years.

It is not known exactly why the use of wool on linen should have become a major feature in 17th century embroidery but perhaps the great expense involved in the purchase of silks and precious threads had forced less wealthy needlewomen to look for a cheaper means of making their bed hangings and furnishings. The wool was home produced and the linen twill often homespun and so allowed a lower strata of society to embellish their homes with decorative embroidery.

The earliest crewel embroideries of the 17th century were often worked in only one colour and although much larger in scale, the designs are very reminiscent of certain blackwork patterns, with coiling stems and tendrils enclosing familiar English flowers. However, it was not long before these crewel embroideries began to reflect influences from much farther afield.

Ever since the expeditions of Marco Polo, and the discoveries of Christopher Columbus, Vasco de Gama and Ferdinand Magellan all Europe had been eager for more knowledge of the new lands and cultures they had reported. From the earliest times, the western world had been fascinated with the Orient and the exotic goods which only it produced. Long before the advent of Christianity, the eminence of the Levant grew out of its fortunate position on the eastern shores of the Mediterranean, from where it controlled the western reaches of the 'silk route'. The silk route, running overland for thousands of miles was, for centuries, the only known connection with the East and the fabulous riches of China. The Vikings are known to have traded in the Levant for the silks and spices which could be obtained nowhere else.

By their very nature, the caravans working the silk route could carry a relatively small amount of goods on their long journeys, thus creating a rarity value which only served to enhance the desirability of the sumptuous silks, spices, perfumes, precious jewels and porcelain which they brought back. Despite the fact that silk worms were smuggled out of China in the 16th century in order to establish a rival silk industry in Italy, the demand for the 'real thing' was in no way diminished. The Levant's control of the lucrative silk route was eventually broken, in 1515, when the Portuguese discovered the first direct sea route to China and established their own trading connections, using ships which could transport Oriental goods in bulk for the first time.

The other great maritime nations, Spain, France and England, seeing the tremendous value of colonising far-off lands were soon vying with each other to expand their mercantile interests abroad. The East India Company was founded by the English in 1600 and in 1613 a charter was granted by the Mughal Emperor, Jahangir, which allowed for an English trading post or 'factory' to be established at Surat, on the mainland of India. It would seem from the correspondence of Sir Thomas Roe, English Ambassador to the Mughal Court, that initially there was some dismay when it was seen that Indian arts and crafts sent back to England were not of the same quality as those to be had from China. The first small cargoes of Indian textiles, despatched with the main shipment of spices for the English market, were probably enjoyed only for their curiosity value. The Indian designs on palampores and pintadoes were not at all what the English had anticipated and did not quite fulfil their desire for the exotic. The research of John Irwin has revealed that what were formerly considered to be pure Indian chintz designs are in fact adaptations which were loosely based on the indigenous designs of India.

After what can be classed as the first exercise in market research, the East India Company discovered what was acceptable to the home market and what could be the most profitable. They employed European artists to adapt the Indian printed, painted and embroidered wall hangings, and to tailor them cleverly to the English taste. It was these designs, developed from a cross-fertilisation of East and West, which took Europe by storm and introduced to English embroiderers a whole range of influences and ideas. Crewel work embroideries soon incorporated all the flavour and imagery of these exciting Indian textiles. Designers created patterns which swirled and curled all over the fabric in what was admired as the height of 'Oriental style'. The repeating patterns of earlier crewel work were put aside in favour of sinuously meandering branches, with huge imaginative leaves and flowers undulating upwards from a hummocky landscape.

Crewel Bedcurtain

Victoria and Albert Museum, London

For colour illustration of project see plate 18

The discoveries in the New World of the Americas also made their mark on crewel work designs. Descriptions of strange, wondrous birds and plants delighted the embroiderers who added them to their patterns alongside lions and tigers, quaintly dressed Chinamen and turbaned hunters. The skill of the Oriental workmanship in the execution of embroidery was greatly admired, and encouraged English needlewomen to aspire to the subtlest shading with long and short stitch, encroaching satin stitch and minute chain stitch.

A wide range of highly decorative laid and couched stitches was developed, perhaps to emulate the tiny patterns found filling leafy shapes on the Indian printed textiles.

The Abigail Pett hangings are a particularly interesting and perhaps unique example of crewel work curtains and valances for a four poster bed. A bed, complete with these hangings, is on permanent exhibition at the Victoria and Albert Museum. The overall design of the embroideries, which have been dated 1675, is not typical of the

The Abigail Pett bed hangings.

general direction of crewel work in the late 17th century, and indeed the rather formal organisation of the separate motifs is more akin to the slip work of the late 16th and early 17th centuries. Nonetheless, the diversity and choice of the flora and fauna which she called upon indicate that Abigail Pett was fully aware of all the prevalent influences of the period. The trees, with their plump leaves have a very tropical quality and grow out of little craggy hummocks of Chinese character. A complete zoo of animals

and birds, both real and fanciful – a camel, lion, stag, dragon, griffon, monkey, and bird of paradise – show how very receptive she was to the tales carried back by explorers and to the current pattern publications. The image of the dragon, amongst others, can be traced to an engraving published by John Overton and Peter Stent, in 1667, *Animalium Quo* (page 103, below).

The crewel work curtain dated 1699 from the Montreal Museum of Fine Art (page 103, above), although worked only some twenty years after the

Crewel bedhanging from the Montreal Museum of Fine Arts.

Abigail Pett embroidered bedhangings, is an excellent example of how quickly crewel embroidery developed towards the free flowing forms more traditionally associated with this type of work.

A dragon from an engraving published by John Overton and Peter Stent.

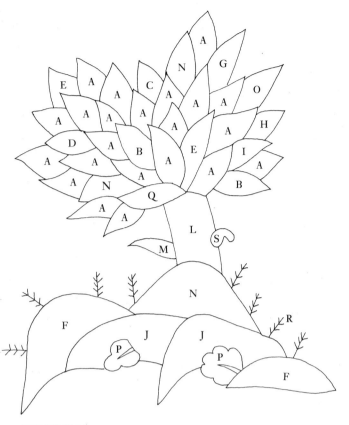

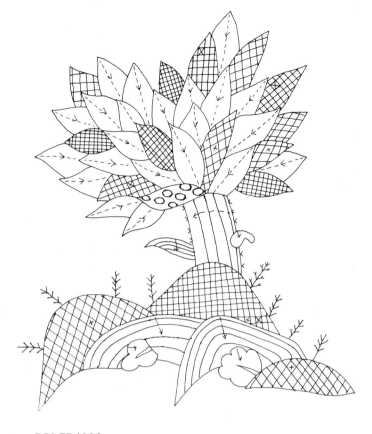

DIAGRAM 1

DIAGRAM 2

A ENCROACHING SATIN FILLING
STITCH 3 ROWS EACH; 331 354
295 158 REMAINING SPACE 328

B SINGLE TRELLIS FILLING
TRELLIS 295
COUCH 225
OUTLINE 331

C SINGLE TRELLIS FILLING
TRELLIS 158
COUCH 225
OUTLINE 331

D SINGLE TRELLIS FILLING
TRELLIS 354
COUCH 225
OUTLINE 331

E DOUBLE TRELLIS FILLING
TRELLIS 158
COUCH 331
CROSS 225
OUTLINE 331

F DOUBLE TRELLIS FILLING

    TRELLIS 295
    COUCH 331
    CROSS 225
    OUTLINE 354

G DOUBLE TRELLIS FILLING
TRELLIS 158
COUCH 331
CROSS 295
OUTLINE 331

H DOUBLE TRELLIS FILLING
WITH SATIN STITCH
TRELLIS 295
COUCH 331
SATIN STITCH 158
OUTLINE 331

I DOUBLE TRELLIS FILLING
TRELLIS 295
COUCH 331
CROSS 158
OUTLINE 331

J STEM STITCH FILLING
331 354 295 158 328

L OUTLINE STITCH FILLING
902 764 303 905 181

M OUTLINE STITCH FILLING
331 354 295 158 328

N BRICK AND CROSS STITCH FILLING
SPLIT STITCH 295
SATIN STITCH 354
CROSS 158
OUTLINE 331

O BRICK AND CROSS STITCH FILLING
SATIN STITCH 354
CROSS 225
OUTLINE 331

P LONG AND SHORT STITCH FILLING
331 354 295 158 328
CENTRE 902 303 581

Q SATIN STITCH 158

R OUTLINE 295
FEATHER 295
FEATHER 225

S STEM STITCH 902 303 581

Abigail Pett bed hanging. Finished size 11½″ × 10″. Stitches used: encroaching satin stitch, outline stitch, stem stitch, feather stitch, satin stitch, laid and couched fillings. Worked on linen twill, using one strand of Appleton's crewel wool. Diagram 1 shows pattern outline together with the key for stitches and colours; diagram 2 shows guidelines, stitch directions and arrows for working from light to dark.

Crewel Hanging

Littlecote House, Berkshire

For colour illustration of project see plate 19

Crewel coverlet from Littlecote House showing the influence of Indian motifs.

COLOURS USED

DRAB GREEN 332
GREY GREEN 355
DULL ROSE PINK 145
BRIGHT TERRACOTTA 226
PUTTY 984
TERRACOTTA 127
MID OLIVE 342
JACOBEAN 294
MID OLIVE 348
OLIVE 241
MID BLUE 157
MID BLUE 155
DULL CHINA 929
PEACOCK 643

KEY TO CHART
A ALL SMALL LEAVES

DULL CHINA 929
MID BLUE 153
MID BLUE 157
PEACOCK 643
MID OLIVE 342
INFILLING, ROWS OF STEM STITCH
STARTING AT OUTER EDGE WITH
DARKEST BLUE

B LARGE STALK

B1 GREY GREEN 355
B2 DRAB GREEN 332
B3 MID OLIVE 348
ENCROACHING SATIN STITCH

C CHERRIES

BRIGHT TERRACOTTA 226
STEM STITCH INFILLING

LARGE LEAF

VEINS

D DULL CHINA 929
E PEACOCK 643
STEM STITCH, FRENCH KNOTS
AND SPECKLING

F LEAF STEM AND INNER LEAVES

DULL CHINA 929
MID BLUE 157
PEACOCK 643
MID OLIVE 342
STEM STITCH, INFILLING COLOURS
GRADED DARK
TO LIGHT ON LEAVES STARTING
WITH DARKEST
TONE AT OUTER EDGE

G LARGE LEAF TIP

DULL CHINA 929
MID BLUE 157
PEACOCK 643
MID BLUE 153
MID OLIVE 342
STEM STITCH INFILLING

H CURLED EDGES

1   MID OLIVE 342
2   PEACOCK 643
3   DULL CHINA 929
LONG AND SHORT, STEM
AND SPECKLING STITCHES

J BIRD

LONG FEATHERS
OLIVE 241
FEATHER STITCH

K WINGS

DULL ROSE PINK 145
MID BLUE 155
MID BLUE 157
DRAB GREEN 332

The practice of hanging painted canvas on interior walls in imitation of verdure tapestries was already well established by the 16th century in manor houses in England and a fine example can be seen lining a room at Packwood House. Indian palampores featuring the 'tree of life' motif with its rich luxuriant imagery of flowering trees inhabited by phoenixes, birds of paradise, parrots and animals of the forest, presented a wonderfully colourful alternative and made handsome panels which instantly enriched any interior.

This embroidered hanging on display at Littlecote House is an excellent example of early 18th century crewel work. It illustrates the zenith of the Indian influence on English crewel embroidery and the fullest development of the technique. Boldly striped branches of the Tree of Life meander throughout the length and breadth of the linen twill ground. They bear large serrated leaves worked in subtly shaded outline stitch and filled with a filligree of coral stitch giving them a light airiness. Between the leaves the most beautifully decorative birds of paradise, peacocks, and parrots peck at cherries and rosebuds amidst delicate flowers of all kinds. The 'Tree of Life' adapted easily to any large scale work, its branches able to extend as far as the designer needed. By the use of quick and easy basic crewel stitches – long and short, satin, coral, herringbone, french knots and buttonhole stitch the embroidery could be accomplished with relative speed. Since the patterns were not required to follow any preconceived notions of design other than that of free-flowing liveliness, the embroiderers had considerable scope to use their imagination in developing infilling patterns and their own colour harmonies.

Littlecote crewel coverlet. Embroidery worked on linen twill
cloth using Appletons crewel wool in stem stitch,
encroaching satin stitch, French knots, long and short stitch,
feather stitch and speckling. Finished size approximately
12″ × 14″.

Crewel Bedcover

Metropolitan Museum of Art, New York

For colour illustration of project see plate 16

England's first colony was established in North American in 1585 by Sir Walter Raleigh. He named the settlement Virginia in deference to his Queen, Elizabeth I 'the virgin Queen'. However, this first settlement was later wiped out and it was not until three years after Elizabeth's death, when in 1606 a trading colony was re-established in Virginia that a permanent community began there. The early colonists were mainly people of good birth, who sailed to the New World to increase their fortunes and to do their patriotic duty. They took with them the traditions and, as far as was possible, the life style of the English gentry.

In 1620, a small group of Puritans left England aboard the *Mayflower* bound for America. The Pilgrim Fathers stemmed from varying social backgrounds but all were united in seeking refuge from the growing religious intolerance pervading England. They established the territories of New England and were at last free to practise their faith without fear of oppression. The emnity and fear in England between Catholic and Protestant was further inflamed by the marriage of Charles I to the Catholic Henrietta Maria of France. The ensuing strife and eventual civil war swelled the flood of emigrants to the New World and by the end of the century all but one of the territories which made up New England had been established as English colonies.

The later emigrants were a little more fortunate than the first, for letters of warning, sent from the colonising companies in America, urged them to bring enough necessities to see them safely through the initial hardships. Certainly amongst the few precious belongings they were able to take with them were examples of needlework patterns and a few materials with which to work them. There are very few surviving crewel embroideries in America dating from the 17th century and it is impossible to be certain whether those that do exist were made there or in England. Even those which may have been worked in the colonies were based on English designs, using English wools and linen.

Examples of 18th century American crewel embroideries indicate that they soon displayed a character of their own and were much less dependent on England for their inspiration. The embroideries of New England are distinctly different from their English counterparts, with a much lighter and airier treatment of motifs. This may at first have arisen purely from necessity, as wools and linen were still being imported from England so the cost was very high and only those living in or near the towns had a ready access to them. The colonists, who always encouraged keen frugality, developed crewel work designs which were economical, and stitches such as flat stitch, Roumanian couching and economy stitch which used as little wool as possible. The resulting embroideries, far from looking skimped or empty, have an innate elegance and a restraint which is very attractive indeed. Certain motifs enjoyed great popularity, perhaps sponsored by the few ladies' magazines which were published in

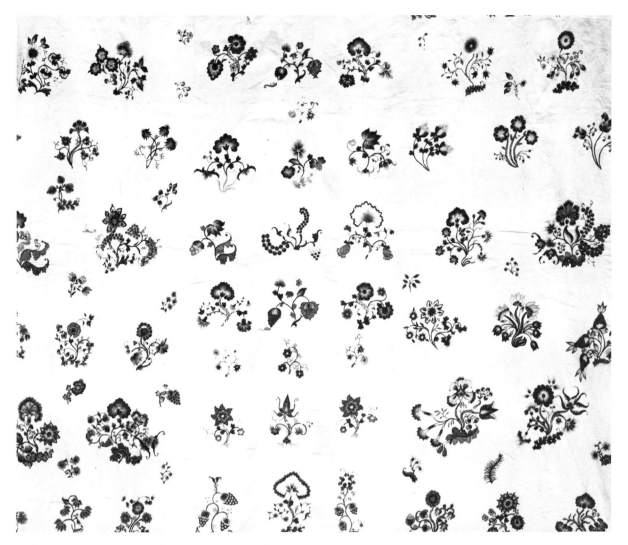

18th century American crewel bedcover by Lucinda Coleman, now in the Metropolitan Museum, New York.

America in the late 18th century. Alongside patterns displaying the latest fashions from England were designs based on images much closer to home. Many of the trees, fruits and animals were a familiar part of the surrounding countryside.

The crewel embroidered coverlet from the Metropolitan Museum in New York featured here is part of the set of bed furnishings worked by Lucinda Coleman in the 18th century. This coverlet, worked in Roumanian couching, bullion, outline weaving and economy stitch displays carefully arranged sprigs of flowers and berries. The use of weaving stitches in the leaves and parts of the cornflowers is particularly interesting and was perhaps inspired by the work of neighbouring settlers of Scandinavian origin. Each of the motifs is worked in shades of light and dark blue and the inventive use of the stitches adds rich texture. The very pleasing visual harmony of the design, though immediately recognisable as American, has in fact its counterpart in England, where a small group of crewel embroideries emulated the tiny, block printed sprig patterns of India (page 111).

Crewel coverlet from the Metropolitan Museum of Art. Finished size $14\frac{1}{2}'' \times 9''$. Worked in Roumanian couching stitch, economy stitch, outline stitch, and patterns of darning stitch on heavy linen, using one strand of Appleton's crewel wool. For clarity, the designs have been separated in this pattern.

A
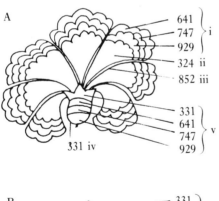

641
747 } i
929
324 ii
852 iii

331
641
747 } v
929

331 iv

E
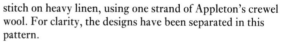

324 i
852 ii

852 v

929 iii
852 iv

B

331
641 } i
747
929

929 } iii
331

331 ii

F
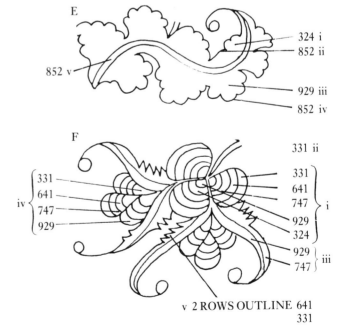

331 ii

331
641 } iv
747
929

331
641
747 } i
929
324

929 } iii
747

v 2 ROWS OUTLINE 641
331

110

English 18th century crewelwork curtain from The Victoria and Albert Museum.

A i and iv ECONOMY STITCH
   ii CHEVRON DARNING PATTERN A
   iii and iv OUTLINE STITCH

B i and iii (929) ECONOMY STITCH
   ii and iii (331) OUTLINE STITCH

C i ROUMANIAN COUCHING STITCH
   ii OUTLINE STITCH

D i and iii ECONOMY STITCH
   ii CHAIN STITCH

E i CHEQUER DARNING PATTERN B
   ii and iv OUTLINE STITCH
   iii STRIPED DARNING PATTERN C
   v OUTLINE FILLING STITCH

F i, iii and iv ECONOMY STITCH
   ii and iii OUTLINE STITCH

G i ROUMANIAN COUCHING STITCH
   ii and iii OUTLINE STITCH

H i ECONOMY STITCH
   ii OUTLINE STITCH

I i ROUMANIAN COUCHING STITCH
   ii OUTLINE STITCH

MAIN STEM AND SMALLER BRANCHES ALL
WORKED IN ROWS OF OUTLINE STITCH
WITH 852

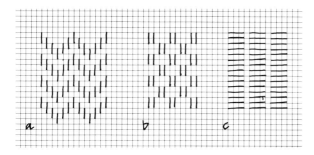

Patterns for darning stitches.

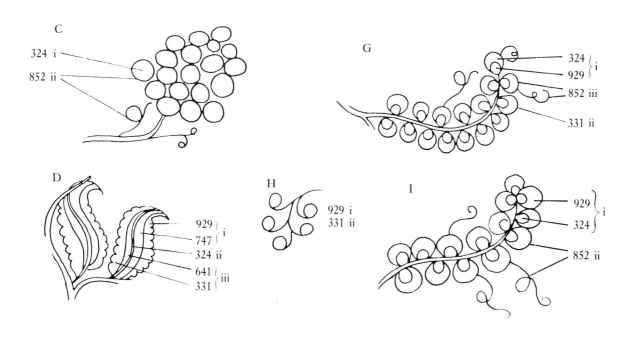

C
324 i
852 ii

G
324 } i
929 }
852 iii
331 ii

D
929 } i
747 }
324 ii
641 } iii
331 }

H
929 i
331 ii

I
929 } i
324 }
852 ii

8 FLORENTINE

The origins of florentine needlework lie in the brick stitch used in much early medieval embroidery. A similar surface pattern of chevron lines is also found formed by underside couching stitch (a method of anchoring silk and gold thread to a base fabric). During the renowned period of Opus Anglicanum embroidery, these techniques were favoured for covering large background areas and it was the perfect foil to the intensity and richness of the figurative elements which were the main feature of those embroideries. Florentine embroidery, with its distinctive flame-like patterns achieved by a simple upright stitch and subtle gradation of colour, would appear to be a direct development from these medieval embroideries. The simplicity of the florentine stitch and its economic use of the wool or silk (covering up to six or eight threads of the canvas at once) was attractive to embroiderers of all eras. The development of the characteristic zig-zag lines, the flame pattern, carnation or ogee, was motivated by the freedom to exploit colour to the full not only in bands of the finest gradations but also in sizzling colour combinations which made the surface of the embroidery excitingly vital.

It would seem that Italian needleworkers were amongst the first to see the potential of this form of embroidery and from the 16th century onwards they were extremely creative in their production of fine hangings and coverings which found their way all over Europe. At the turn of the 17th century in England, large florentine stitch wallhangings, and complete bed furnishings were rare but greatly admired and treasured imports from Italy. There are now but a few pieces left, but their very existence is proof of how desirable the English found these wonderful embroideries.

One of the most exquisite examples of 16th century Italian florentine work can be seen at Parham Park, Sussex. A glorious bed, complete with florentine embroidered curtains and valances, worked in the traditional flame pattern using Hungarian stitch, features rich bands of glowing wools and silks in greens, browns, terracottas, golds and ivory, cleverly graded against each other to create a texture and surface of remarkable elegance.

The religious and political upheavals which beleaguered England from the second quarter of the 17th century created an atmosphere which was not at all conducive to the undertaking of much large-scale work. Civil war and the eventual beheading of Charles I left the country for eleven years under the protection of the Commonwealth government of Oliver Cromwell. However, even during this troubled and often austere period, embroidery remained popular and plentiful, but with a marked preference for small scale items such as Bible covers, purses, embroidered pictures, caskets and samplers. Florentine embroidery had none the less begaun to enter the consciousness of the English embroiderer. Three samplers dating from about 1600 in the Carew-

Pole collection are devoted entirely to florentine patterns, indicating that English embroiderers were well acquainted with the working of the stitches and patterns of florentine embroidery at an early date.

A quite distinct group of English florentine embroideries, with examples displayed at Packwood House, Parham Park and Chastleton House, dating from the early 17th century, remain a paradox. At first glance these hangings all appear to have been stitched in a regular florentine manner. It is only on close inspection that they reveal the use of a slightly different stitch – one that is worked diagonally on the canvas rather than upright, producing a surface which resembles that of a knitted stitch.

From the mid-17th century weavers in Northern France and Flanders using the hand draw loom were able to produce a woven textile based on the flame stitch patterns which was virtually indistinguishable from this type of embroidered work. Only by looking at the back of the fabric can the weaving by detected, although the 'stitches' tend to be looser and a little coarser than the embroidered florentine.

An ante-room at Chastleton House has magnificent wall coverings, reaching from floor to ceiling, embroidered in this early form of English florentine. These hangings are reputed to have been worked 'on the spot' and certainly look made to measure. Those at Parham Park are remarkably similar in stitch and choice of colours and perhaps came originally from the same source. It is difficult to place this group in a category other than its own and one can only guess at the reasons for the variation in the stitch. Perhaps it was a slightly misunderstood interpretation of the Italian work or simply a quicker way of covering the canvas on such ambitious projects. Certainly by the end of the 17th century the naturally eclectic English embroiderers had mastered the art of florentine embroidery and utilised it magnificently in their work.

With the restoration of the monarchy in 1660, England looked forward with optimism to a gradual return to a peaceful existence. Catholics who had sought asylum abroad during the Commonwealth, returned to their homes and people throughout the country settled down to the renewal of their estates. Despite the setbacks of the great plague and the fire of London, there was time at last to savour in depth the diversity of influences brought into England by returning exiles and by the growth of trade abroad.

Although the new vogue for crewel work permeated everywhere, a general revival of interest in large-scale embroidery allowed for a separate development in canvas embroidery. The upsurge in florentine embroidery at the end of the 17th century, during the reign of William and Mary, ran concurrently with that of crewel work and both played a major part in the decorative scheme of the day.

Mary, daughter of the banished James II, came to the English throne with her husband William of Orange following Parliament's suggestion that they should rule together. Thus Holland and England were jointly ruled by William and Mary and England was brought into the closest and most immediate contact with continental influences. The style and culture of Holland soon entered into the arts and crafts of England, influencing architecture, paintings, interior arrangements, furniture and of course, embroidery. For the English embroiderer, Dutch flower paintings proved to be the most valuable source of inspiration which manifested itself in a quite distinct form of florentine design, where crewel work stitches and florentine stitches came together in a most exciting way. Vast swags of flowers and leaves, bouquets tied with ribbons, and urns brimming with foliage and fruit were worked in a free mix of florentine stitch, Hungarian stitch, long and short shading and french knots. The use of florentine stitch to create floral rather than purely geometric designs was not entirely new and no doubt the English designers had seen Italian embroideries of this nature which employed very baroque and neoclassical features. However, the flower paintings of Holland brought a hitherto

The State bed at Clandon Park.

The state bed at Drayton House uses this figurative development of florentine embroidery in the most magnificent hangings of the late 17th or early 18th century. The Dutch influence is felt in the wide variety of flowers and foliage flowing out of the decorative vases and reaching up the extraordinary height of the bed. Worked in naturalistic colours against a dark background the design matches the grandeur and majestic scale of the bed itself.

The state bed at Clandon Park in Surrey (left) shows a similar use of this type of embroidery, but here the design would appear to owe more to the oriental influence. These impressive hangings, with a set of chairs *en suite* are worked in a wonderful blend of wool and silk. The variation in texture created by laying wool against silk, combined with the changes in direction of the florentine stitches, give an added dimension to the leaves and flowers. The overall richness and life this brings to the surface was an aspect of some importance when dealing with such large areas of embroidery. The freedom of design achieved with the use of florentine, Hungarian and various crewel stitches on this large scale is a monument to the technical skill of the professional embroiderer involved. It is indeed a delight to find bed furnishings worked in this style of florentine, so complete and in such handsome settings as Drayton House and Clandon Park. These must have been only two of many state beds adorned in this way, for existing fragments indicate a wide use of this particular style of embroidery.

unexplored range of flower motifs to the English interpretation of floral florentine embroidery designs.

With the new influences in architecture, the rooms of great houses were built on a very grand scale with high ceilings and ornate features. State apartments, prepared in readiness for any impending royal visit were an extremely important part of the homes of the wealthy. Enormous expense was lavished on state beds which became tall and elegant to match their imposing surroundings. These beds, conceived by artists such as Daniel Marot (a Frenchman who had worked for the Dutch royal house before settling in England) had hangings which were an integral part of the design, fitting perfectly with the very architectural concept of the beds.

114

Florentine Valance

Cooper-Hewitt Museum, New York

For colour illustration of project see plate 20

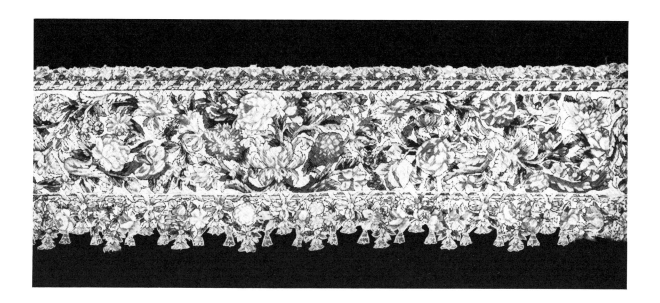

This piece is all that remains of a further set of hangings worked in a mixture of crewel and florentine stitches. It is a perfect example displaying the wide range of design influences which were at the embroiderer's disposal at this time. The valance is composed of a variety of flowers – roses, tulips, chrysanthemums, peonies, carnations, daffodils and forget-me-nots. The choice of peonies and chrysanthemums, so much a feature of the piece, reflects the influence of the Orient, yet the borders with their swags of dainty blossoms interlaced with ribbons and bows clearly owe more to the tradition of French and Italian design. The rich warm pinks, browns, yellows and terracottas of the flowers and the blue-greens of the acanthus leaves, worked both in wool and silk, are elegantly set off by the lightest gold silk of the background.

115

Valance from the Cooper-Hewitt museum. Embroidery worked with 2 strands Appleton's crewel wool and 6 strands of DMC and Anchor embroidery cotton on 18 gauge canvas using florentine stitch, French knots and outlined in back stitch. Border repeat size approximately $7'' \times 4\frac{1}{2}''$.

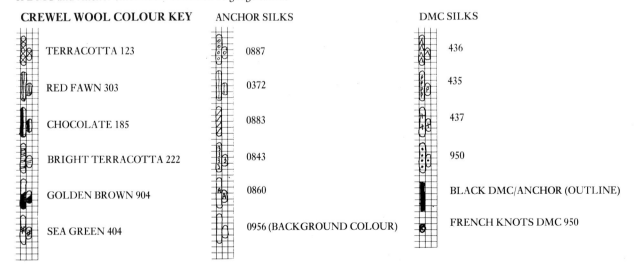

CREWEL WOOL COLOUR KEY	ANCHOR SILKS	DMC SILKS
TERRACOTTA 123	0887	436
RED FAWN 303	0372	435
CHOCOLATE 185	0883	437
BRIGHT TERRACOTTA 222	0843	950
GOLDEN BROWN 904	0860	BLACK DMC/ANCHOR (OUTLINE)
SEA GREEN 404	0956 (BACKGROUND COLOUR)	FRENCH KNOTS DMC 950

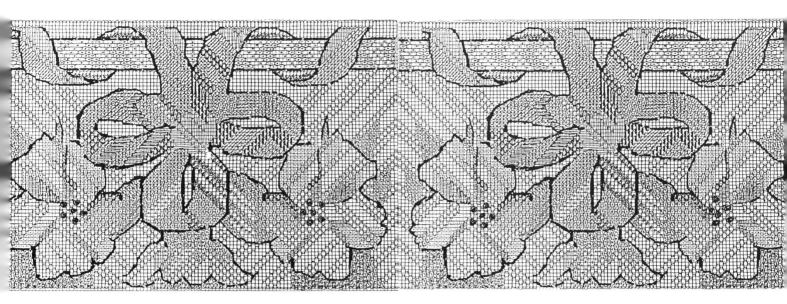

Chart indicating how design repeats to form a border.

Queen Anne Chair

Parham Park, Sussex

For colour illustration of project see plate 21

A third group of English florentine embroideries followed the more traditional lines of the purely geometric shapes of the Italian manner. The basic characteristics of the florentine stitch made it a most attractive choice for embroiderers embarking on the coverings for upholstered furniture which was increasingly popular in the English home. This Queen Anne chair from Parham Park (opposite page) exemplifies how the inventive juxtaposition of silk and wool in a relatively simple florentine pattern could achieve great beauty. In the candlelit rooms of the 18th

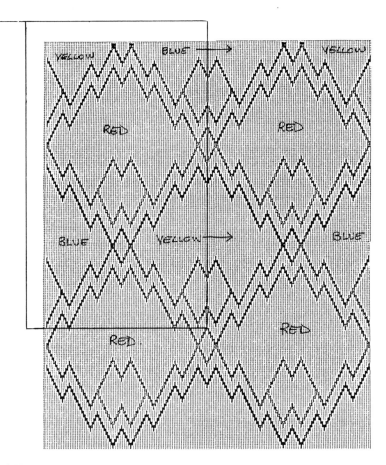

Outline chart for the full embroidery. The charted section is marked.

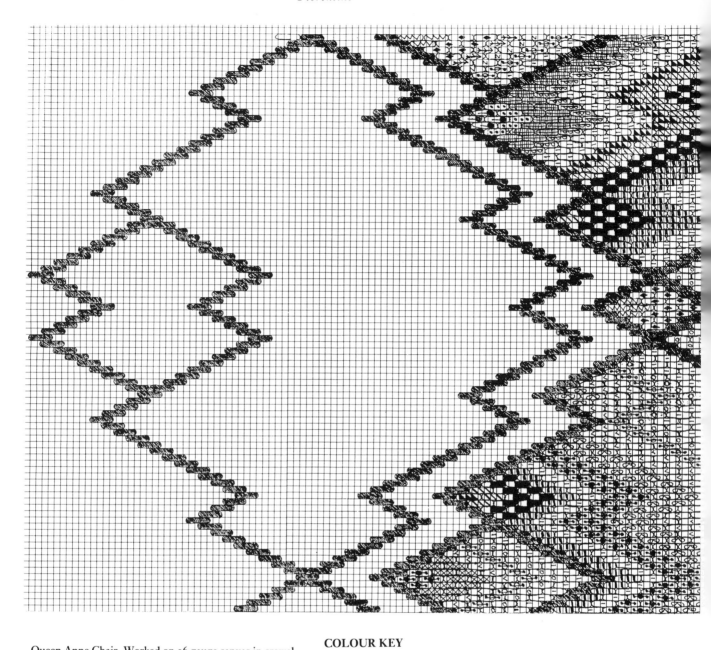

Queen Anne Chair. Worked on 16 gauge canvas in crewel wool and silk using florentine stitch. Approximate finished size 12″ × 15″.

COLOUR KEY

APPLETONS CREWEL WOOL

DRAB GREEN 337

OLIVE GREEN 241

DRAB FAWN 951

HONEYSUCKLE 695

DRAB GREEN 332

MID BLUE 155

FLAME 207

MID BLUE 156

DULL MARINE 326

DULL ROSE PINK 142

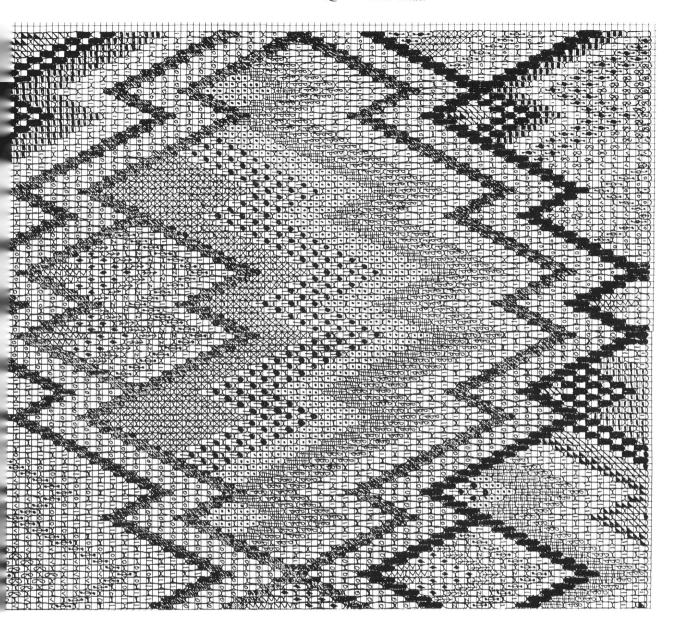

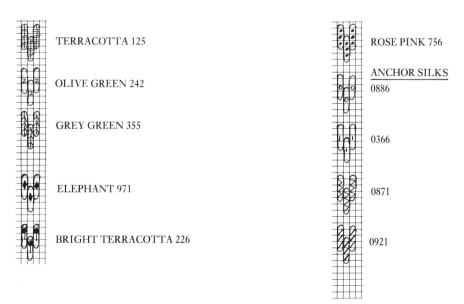

TERRACOTTA 125

OLIVE GREEN 242

GREY GREEN 355

ELEPHANT 971

BRIGHT TERRACOTTA 226

ROSE PINK 756

ANCHOR SILKS

0886

0366

0871

0921

Woven cushion from Trondheim.

and 19th centuries, chairs with this type of florentine covers must have been very warm and inviting.

Florentine embroidery was well received all over Europe and wherever needlework was practised, florentine patterns made their mark. In Scandinavia, where weaving was a stronger tradition among the peasant artisans than embroidery, the zig-zag patterns were translated to fit their weaving technique. Their northern predilection for bright and vibrant colour made the florentine format an ideal one for them, allowing for a thorough exploration of new combinations and groupings of colours. This resulted in some astonishingly beautiful pieces. A group of cushion covers from the district of Skåne in Sweden shows 18th century adaptations of the florentine patterns. The cushion from the Kunstindustrimuseum in Trondheim, Norway (photograph above) is a fine example of how the woven variation of florentine was produced in the north where it was known as the 'lightning pattern'.

German samplers of the 18th and 19th century display a wide variety of the florentine patterns and the dolls house in the Rijksmuseum, Amsterdam, has a complete room worked in a tiny version of flame stitch.

Chasuble

Cooper-Hewitt Museum, New York

For colour illustration of project see plate 22

Florentine naturally made its way across the Atlantic to America where it was quickly established as a favourite form of embroidery for all manner of projects from carpets, window and bed hangings to small pocket books, hand screens and shoes, as well as for the coverings of upholstered furniture. The range and variety of patterns produced in America is vast indeed but one of the most fascinating pieces is a table carpet in the Henry Dupont Winterthur Museum, Delaware (photograph below). It was worked in 1759 by Mary Oothout and displays a most

Tablecarpet from the Henry Dupont Winterthur Museum.

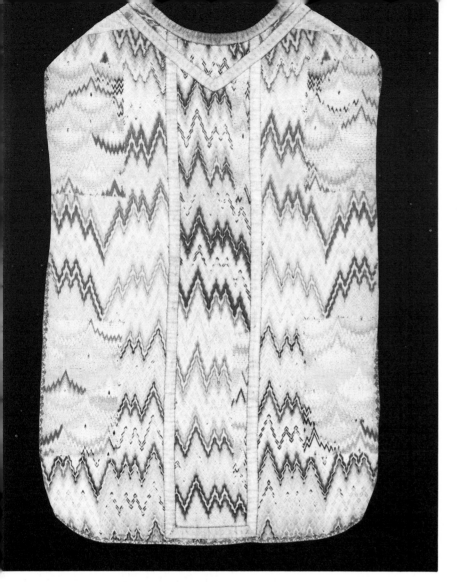

19th century chasuble from the Cooper-Hewitt Museum, combining two different florentine patterns. The embroidery itself is 17th or 18th century.

Opposite. Chasuble from the Cooper-Hewitt Museum. Finished size $8\frac{1}{2}'' \times 11\frac{3}{4}''$. Worked in florentine stitch and hungarian stitch on canvas, 24 threads to the inch, using 6 strands of Anchor and DMC stranded embroidery cotton. For the florentine part follow the fully charted area. The partly charted areas of the hungarian pattern are to indicate how the stitches fall. To check that the pattern is falling correctly, the stitch count vertically should be the same as that diagonally, i.e. 1 long stitch : 3 short stitches.

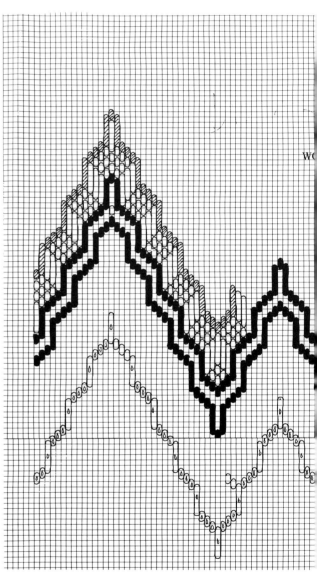

COLOUR KEY

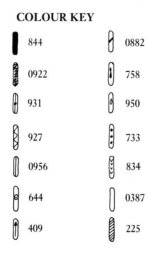

844		0882	
0922		758	
931		950	
927		733	
0956		834	
644		0387	
409		225	

(ii) COLOUR SEQUENCE FOR SECTION A

RUNNING UP FROM (i)	RUNNING DOWN FROM (i)		
1 × 844	1 × 0956	2 × 0956	1 × 758
3 × 0387	1 × 844	1 × 844	2 × 950
2 × 225	3 × 0387	1 × 0956	6 × 038
2 × 950	2 × 225	1 × 844	1 × 844
2 × 224	2 × 950	2 × 0956	1 × 095
1 × 221	2 × 224	2 × 0372	1 × 844
1 × 0378	3 × 221	2 × 0956	6 × 038
2 × 221	2 × 0956	4 × 729	2 × 950
2 × 0956	1 × 435	1 × 435	1 × 758
2 × 0922	4 × 729	2 × 0956	2 × 088
2 × 931	2 × 0956	1 × 407	
2 × 927	2 × 0372	2 × 0882	

FILL TO TOP EDGE 644

124

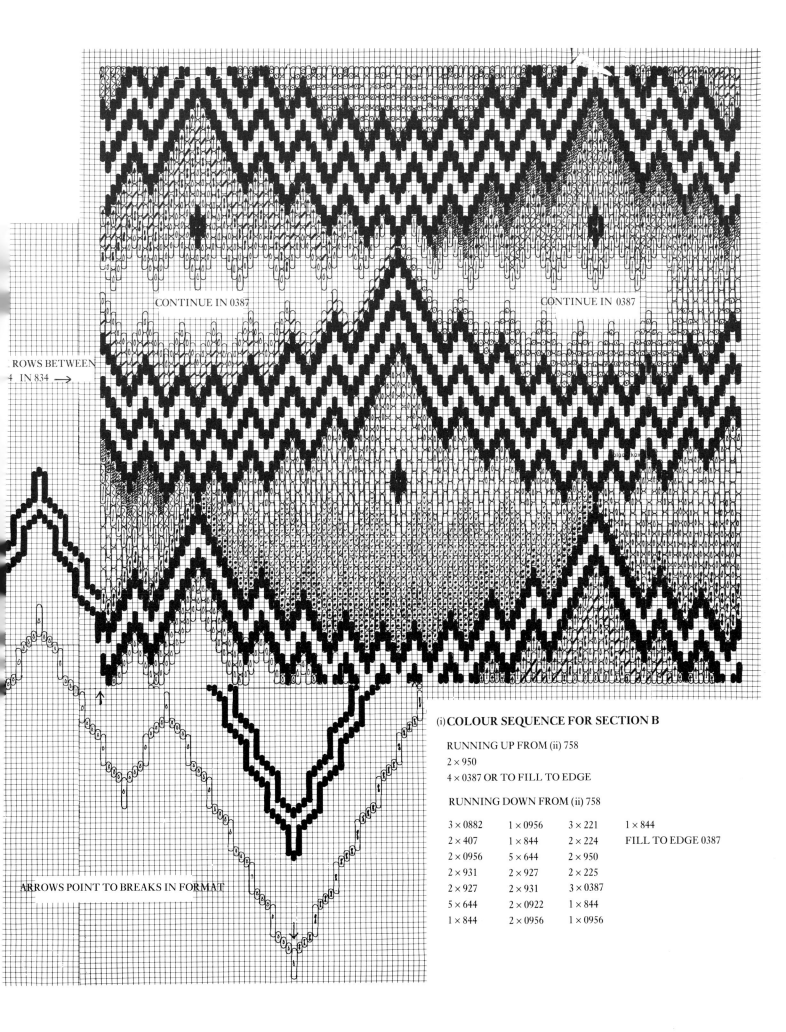

CONTINUE IN 0387

CONTINUE IN 0387

ROWS BETWEEN
4 IN 834 →

ARROWS POINT TO BREAKS IN FORMAT

(i) COLOUR SEQUENCE FOR SECTION B

RUNNING UP FROM (ii) 758

2 × 950

4 × 0387 OR TO FILL TO EDGE

RUNNING DOWN FROM (ii) 758

3 × 0882	1 × 0956	3 × 221	1 × 844
2 × 407	1 × 844	2 × 224	FILL TO EDGE 0387
2 × 0956	5 × 644	2 × 950	
2 × 931	2 × 927	2 × 225	
2 × 927	2 × 931	3 × 0387	
5 × 644	2 × 0922	1 × 844	
1 × 844	2 × 0956	1 × 0956	

imaginative use of several florentine patterns set against each other with the addition of small areas of cross stitch and rice stitch. Miss Oothout quite obviously felt no restraints when designing her embroidery and the resulting cloth has a vibrant originality.

The chasuble from the collection of the Cooper Hewitt Museum also displays this curious break in the design, using two quite separate florentine patterns in the one embroidery. The provenance of this piece is uncertain and although Italian embroiderers produced ecclesiastical garments in florentine stitch, the shell-like pattern incorporated in the design of this piece occurs many times on German samplers. The chasuble was in fact made up in the late 19th century out of what might once have been a covering or hanging, and the lace covering the joins in the fabric are certainly of a much later date than the embroidery itself.

CONCLUSION

The embroideries featured in this book are fine examples which show how, from the earliest times, embroiderers, artists and designers have been eager to accept and assimilate images, styles, techniques and patterns without fear of being branded as copyists. Whatever the source, the embroiderers made their individual responses, adapting or re-creating from a multitude of influences, to create pieces of work which were essentially their own.

Embroidery could be considered as no more than surface decoration, yet it can be seen to have fulfilled a variety of needs. It was used as a tool for promoting ideas by the Church and the state. Embroidered state beds displayed the very essence of status and power for the wealthy, and samplers, with their row upon row of alphabets, were an aid to learning. However, above all, to the majority embroidery was the means by which they could improve and enhance the quality of life within the surroundings of the home.

This rich heritage we have has been established in the way of all good things, through a healthy curiosity of life and a generosity of spirit which allowed for the interchange of ideas. Long may it continue.

BIBLIOGRAPHY

E. A. J. BARNARD AND A. J. B. WACE, *Sheldon Tapestry*, Society of Antiquities 1928.

WILFRID BLUNT, *Splendours of Islam*, Viking Press N.Y. 1976.

HARRIET BRIDGEMAN AND ELIZABETH DRURY, *Needlework – An Illustrated History*, Paddington Press 1971.

MRS ARCHIBALD CHRISTIE, *Samplers and Stitches*, Batsford 1929.

REMBERT DODOENS, *Cruyde Boeck 1554*.

ROSEMARY EWLES, *One Man's Samplers, The Goodhart Collection*, The Embroiderers' Guild.

ERNST FISCHER, *Från Granatäpple till Skybragd*, Norsk Folkemuseums Årbook 1968/9.

ANNE MARIE FRANZEN, *Høylandteppet*.

MARGARET B. FREEMAN, *The Unicorn Tapestries*, Metropolitan Museum of Art/E. Dutton Inc 1976.

LEONHARD FUCHS, *De Historia Stirpium*, Basle 1542.

AGNES GEIJER, *A History of Textile Art*, Pasold Research Fund/Sotherby Parke Bernet Publications 1979.

CONRAD GESNER, 1. *Historia Plantarum*. 2. *Historia Animalium*, Zurich 1555.

MARK GIROUARD, *Hardwick Hall*, National Trust 1976.

ELSA E. GUDJONSSON, *Traditional Icelandic Embroidery*, The Bulletin of the Needle and Bobbin Club Vol 47 nos 1&2 1963.

YVONNE HACKENBROCK, *English and Other Embroideries from the Collection of Irwin Untermeyer*, Thames and Hudson 1960.

MARIA VAN HEMERT, *The Needlework of the Island of Marken, Netherlands Openluchtmuseum*, Arnhem 1978.

THERLE HUGHES, *English Domestic Needlework 1660/1860*, Abbey Fine Arts.

MARCUS B. HUISH, *Samplers and Tapestry Embroideries*, Dover 1970.

CAROL HUMPHREY, *English Samplers at the Fitzwilliam*, The Fitzwilliam Museum 1984.

JOHN IRWIN, *Indo-European Embroidery*, Embroidery, Spring 1959.

JOHN IRWIN AND KATHERINE B. BRETT, *Origins of Chintz*, HMSO 1970.

MARGARET JOURDAIN, *The History of English Secular Embroidery*, Kegan, Paul, Trench Trubner 1910.

A. F. KENDRICK, *English Needlework*, Adam and Charles Black 1933.

THOR B. KIELLAND, *Norsk Billedvev 1550–1800*, Gyldendal Norsk Forlag 1953–1955.

DONALD KING, *Samplers*, HMSO 1960.

ANDRE LEJARD, *French Tapestry*, Paul Elek 1946.

PIETRO ANDREA MATTHIOLI, 1. *Compendium 1572*. 2. *Discoride 1548*.

ALBARTA MEULENBELT NIEUWBURG, *Embroidery Motifs from Dutch Samplers*, Batsford 1974.

J. MILLS, *Small Pattern Holbein Carpets in Western Painting*, Hali 1 no 4 1978.

A. R. MYERS, *England in the Late Middle Ages*, Penguin Books 1971.

J. L. NEVINSON, 1. *Catalogue of English Domestic Embroidery*, HMSO 1938.
2. *Peter Stent and John Overton, publishers of embroidery designs*, Apollo Nov. 1936 XXIV.
3. *An English Herbarium : Embroideries by Bess of Hardwick after the woodcuts of Matthioli*, The National Trust Year Book 1975/6.
4. *The Embroidery Patterns of Thomas Trevelyon*, Walpole Society, Vol 41 1966/68.
5. *English Domestic Embroidery Patterns of the 16th and 17th Centuries*, Walpole Society Vol 28 1939/40.

CARL NORDENFALK, *Celtic and Anglo Saxon Painting*, Chatto and Windus, 1977.

R. PINNER AND J. STANGER, *Kufic Borders on Small Pattern Holbein Carpets*, Hali 1 no 4 1978.

DAVID PIPER, *Holbein the Younger in England*, Offprint from the Journal of the Royal Society of Arts, August 1963.

MARIE SCHUETTE AND SIGRID MULLER-CHRISTENSEN, *Das Stickereiwerk*, Verlag Ernst Wasmuth 1963.

RICHARD SHORLEYKER, *A Schole House for the Needle 1568*.

EDITH A. STANDEN, *The Shepherd's Sweet Lot*, Bulletin of the Metropolitan Museum of Art vol XXVIII no 6 1970.

STENTON/WINGFIELD-DIGBY/NEVINSON/WORMALD, *The Bayeux Tapestry*, Phaidon Press 1965.

BARBARA SNOOK, *Florentine Embroidery*, Scribner, N.Y. 1967.

MARGARET SWAIN, *The Needlework of Mary Queen of Scots*, V.N.R. 1973.

SUSAN B. SWAN, *Plain and Fancy, American Women and their Needlework 1700–1850*, Holt Reinhart and Winston 1977.

DAVID SYLVESTER, *The Eastern Carpet in the Western World from 15th to 17th Century*, Arts Council of Great Britain 1983.

LISA TAYLOR, *Embroidered Samplers in the Collection of the Cooper-Hewitt Museum*, The Smithsonian Institution 1984.

A. J. B. WACE, *English Embroideries Belonging to Sir John Carew-Pole Bart*.

FREDRICK B. WALLEM, *Tæppet fra Høylandets Kirke*, Kristiania, 1911 Mallingske Bogtrykkeri.

GEORGE WINGFIELD-DIGBY, 1. *Elizabethan Embroidery*, Faber and Faber 1963.
2. *The Devonshire Hunting Tapestries*, HMSO 1971.

BONNIE YOUNG, *Needlework by Nuns*, The Bulletin of the Metropolitan Museum of Art Vol XVIII no 1970.

L. ZICKERMAN, *Sveriges Folkliga Textilkonst : Rolakan Aktiebolaget Svensk Litteratur*, Stockholm 1937.